Praise for *Talkability*

'James is a smart and perceptive juggler of words, I'm just hoping he doesn't start writing lyrics.'

Don Black, Oscar-winning lyricist for cinema and musical theatre, partnering notably with John Barry (titles including *Born Free*, *Thunderball*, *Diamonds are Forever*) and Andrew Lloyd Webber (including lyrics for *Sunset Boulevard*)

'Talk is anything but cheap in James Borg's persuasive new book. Instead he demonstrates how "talkability" is an essential life-skill and important counterbalance to today's text-dominated communications.'

Philip Jones, Editor, *The Bookseller*

'Leaves you with the satisfaction of knowing, that by the end of the book, you have taken your communication skills to a whole new level.'

Angela Rippon, TV and radio broadcaster

'He dissects the language we use and our style of speech – offers a plethora of easy-to-understand pointers for how we can all improve. . . Fascinating reading for anyone who wants to be more effective in life — in any social group!'

Gillian Tett, US Managing Editor, *Financial Times* and award-winning columnist

Talkability

Discover the secrets of effective conversation

JAMES BORG

PEARSON

Harlow, England • London • New York • Boston • San Francisco • Toronto • Sydney
Auckland • Singapore • Hong Kong • Tokyo • Seoul • Taipei • New Delhi
Cape Town • São Paulo • Mexico City • Madrid • Amsterdam • Munich • Paris • Milan

Pearson Education Limited
Edinburgh Gate
Harlow CM20 2JE
United Kingdom
Tel: +44 (0)1279 623623
Web: www.pearson.com/uk

First published 2016 (print and electronic)

ISBN: 978-1-292-01364-0 (print)
978-1-292-01366-4 (PDF)
978-1-292-01367-1 (ePub)

British Library Cataloguing-in-Publication Data
A catalogue record for the print edition is available from the British Library

Library of Congress Cataloging-in-Publication Data
A catalog record for the print edition is available from the Library of Congress

10 9 8 7 6 5 4 3 2 1
20 19 18 17 16

Text design by Design Deluxe
Cover design by Two Associates

Print edition typeset in 10/13pt Sabon LT Pro by SPi Global
Print edition printed by Ashford Colour Press Ltd, Gosport

NOTE THAT ANY PAGE CROSS REFERENCES REFER TO THE PRINT EDITION

Contents

About the author

James Borg spends part of his working time as a business consultant and coach and also conducts personal development and business skills workshops covering memory improvement, interpersonal communication, body language and 'mind control'.

With a profound interest in the workings of the human mind, he developed memory techniques at an early age which eventually established him as a 'memory expert'. After becoming interested in magic, he later specialised and performed in the branch of the art known as 'mind magic'.

Influenced by an academic background in economics and psychology, James has spent a lifetime observing the 'mind-body' connection and went on to study the various mind 'therapies' which result in thinking and behavioural change in a person's personal and working life.

His knowledge was honed in a career that spans the spectrum of advertising, sales, marketing, work psychology, training and journalism. He appears on BBC radio and contributes to national newspapers and magazines on the subject of consumer affairs, body language and business and communication skills. In 2009 he was chosen as a *Harvard Business Review* contributor. He still finds time to pursue occasional travel and sports journalism, which he became involved with early on in his career.

James is the author of the 'trilogy' comprising the Number 1 international bestseller *Persuasion,* the award-winning *Body Language* and *Mind Power,* which have been translated into more than 35 languages.

Persuasion spent a record-breaking 118 consecutive weeks at No 1 in the WHSmith Travel Business chart. In 2013 *Future* magazine published the '50 Best Business Books' of all time, which included *Persuasion* (James being one of only three UK authors to make the list, along with Sir Richard Branson and Sir James Dyson).

Author's acknowledgements

I feel like one of those Oscar winners, standing on stage clutching the golden statuette with both hands and thanking a multitude of people . . .

Talking of which, my thanks to Don Black, Oscar-winning lyricist (famous, amongst other things, for his 007 collaborations with John Barry and musical partnerships with Andrew Lloyd Webber). With a busy schedule of composing words, that hasn't stopped for fifty years and in the middle of new productions – including the return of *Sunset Boulevard* to the London stage – I'm grateful that he took the time to read the manuscript. Also to the delightful Angela Rippon who in the middle of filming a new BBC series and a round of media interviews, made time to read the manuscript and kindly contributed a Foreword for the book. My thanks also to Philip Jones, the esteemed Editor of the book industry's weekly 'bible' *The Bookseller* magazine. Although frenetically busy while processing the shortlists for The British Book Industry Awards 2016, he made an exception and read the proof manuscript and provided a contribution. Also, my thanks to the preview titles editor, Caroline Sanderson who picked this book as a 'personal favourite' and featured it as her 'Editor's Choice' in the magazine. I'm grateful to Gillian Tett, US Managing Editor of the *Financial Times* who in between her busy day-to-day New York activities, her writing and stateside travels, read the manuscript – with my deadline in mind – and contributed her thoughts.

Thanks as always to the Pearson publishing team. A special mention to Laura – Senior Project Editor – one of the last links in the chain after the manuscript is handed over for copyediting. I've worked with her on my books over a period of thirteen years and I commend her for a continual display of patience, politeness and perspicacity. She's taking her talents elsewhere and I wish her good fortune.

Finally, I'm grateful to my wife for putting up with me –again – during the writing of this latest book. The 'thinking' time is as time-consuming as the actual writing time, I always find. (As those of you who have written a book may know, it doesn't end even after the manuscript is handed in. There's a lot more to do after that for months ahead). The process always results in her having to endure the same things as far as she's concerned: periods of absences; my distraction; being preoccupied; poor listening; 'mindlessness'. Oh, and occasional absent-mindedness. (*Now, where did I leave that Oscar?*).

Publisher's acknowledgements

Picture Credits

The publisher would like to thank the following for their kind permission to reproduce their photographs:

(Key: b-bottom; c-centre; l-left; r-right; t-top)

Page 3: **Dan Piraro**; page 222 **Rex Shutterstock:** Everett Collection / REX Shutterstock; page 256 Shutterstock/Alena Kozlova

All other images © Pearson Education

Cartoons

Matt cartoon on page 27 © Telegraph Media Group Limited 2013.

Text

Poetry on page 29 from *Conkers: Poems*, Oxford University Press, USA (Wade, B. 1989) Oxford University Press, USA; Extract on pages 216-7 from 'Are women being held back by too much smiling?', *London Evening Standard*, 17/03/2015 (Sands, S.), London Evening Standard; Article on page 219 from Joanna Lumley's Life Lessons, *The Times*, 19/04/2014 (Deborah Ross).

Author's note
An 'adventure' with words

After completing the 'trilogy', there was another book that I knew I had to write at some stage – a book on 'talk'. Otherwise, as far as I was concerned, it was 'unfinished business'. It had been in my mind long before and I made it my aim to bring this to fruition at some time.

I've always been interested in – and studied – 'psycholinguistics'. Specifically the element of linguistics that deals with how words affect our *mind* and *emotions;* the mental processes of how we use language and the relationship between language and thought. Newer, non-invasive brain-imaging techniques such as fMRI (functional magnetic resonance imaging) have now helped us to study further the cognitive processes related to spoken language.

People that I come across and delegates on courses and workshops have suggested to me – over the years – some topics that they would like to see covered, as well as revealing their personal frustrations about communication in everyday life. In addition, the comments I've received during research group sessions have been revealing.

What's interesting is that as far as topics that were suggested, very little has changed. I've covered areas that seem to cause the most problems in our everyday dealings in our personal and working lives.

We seem to have the same difficulties: poor or lazy speaking habits, disagreements, misunderstandings, apologising, giving praise/accepting it, relaying criticism . . . the list is endless. In addition, what was striking were the frustrations that many people mentioned when dealing with the medical profession and the continuing distrust of what politicians say and do. There's a 'silver lining' here. We can look at the 'deficiencies' that we recognise in them and therefore help ourselves in the way we communicate with others – to inspire more trust.

My own experiences in everyday life and the working world of clients, meetings and presentations over the decades has obviously been fertile ground. I confess to a certain amount of unintended 'eavesdropping' on people's conversations, which has also been extremely helpful.

Make a decision to change your habits and feel the excitement of going on an 'adventure' with words. As I state repeatedly, habits take time to change.

Eventually, this quest to explore a new way of talking will prove to be a worthwhile journey. It will make life more interesting, satisfying and less stressful. It will certainly change relationships. *It will certainly change your life.*

So look at your speaking habits and take an objective look at how your talking skills can be improved. Consider how *single* words or a different *turn of phrase* can change outcomes – good or bad.

You can dip into various chapters in Part Two or read the book from start to finish. I've cross-referred chapters where appropriate, to elaborate on a point.

I remember a singer improvising on the words of a song in which she sang about how – in our lifetime – we go through different stages: 'You grow/you learn/you try to turn the pages . . .'

After turning these pages I hope I will have inspired you to go on and take the risk of exploring your 'adventure' with words. Explore the use of alternative words and phrases and notice the different outcomes.

As Paulo Coelho said:

'If you think adventure is dangerous, try routine; it is lethal.'

Foreword

by Angela Rippon

James Borg is clearly a man who understands the wisdom of the saying 'words are free, it's how you use them that might cost you.'

In this his latest 'adventure with words' he explores the power of the spoken word; guides you through the minefield of getting the tone and content just right in domestic, professional and social conversations. And leaves you with the satisfaction of knowing, that by the end of the book, you have taken your communication skills to a whole new level.

Angela Rippon has been a familiar face and voice in British broadcasting for over 40 years. Her career, after training as a journalist in her home town of Plymouth, embraces an impressive variety of programmes for both radio and television in Britain, America and Australia.

She was appointed the first woman journalist newsreader of BBC One's Nine O'Clock News *in 1975. Since then she has presented a wide variety of programmes from hard news and current affairs, to quiz shows and magazine programmes for both BBC and commercial radio and television. In 1981 she co-presented the BBC's coverage of the wedding of the Prince of Wales and Lady Diana Spencer.*

Currently, she presents BBC's Rip Off Britain *and reports for* The One Show *on BBC One as well as presenting the BBC series,* How to Stay Young. *Other credits include hosting the series* Come Dancing *and she was the first ever presenter of* Top Gear.

"So difficult is it to show the various meanings and imperfections of words when we have nothing else but words to do it with."

JOHN LOCKE

PART ONE

Talk essentials

Introduction

I

'Feel the magic in the making . . .'

'Of course there must be lots of magic in the world', he said wisely one day, 'but people don't know what it is like or how to make it. Perhaps the beginning is to say nice things are going to happen until you make them happen. I am going to try and experiment.'

Francis Hodgson Burnett, *The Secret Garden*

The words you use determine your success in your life, relationships, job and business. Those who understand the power of the spoken word and how it affects the hearts and minds of people will have made a conscious decision to develop their speaking skills.

Most of our educational systems don't teach how important words are in our daily conversations and how they shape our reality. You'll often hear metaphorical statements about 'the magic of words'. Yet there is true magic in the way that words create situations and responses.

We cast spells with our language.

Is there something in the fact that the word 'spell' has a twin meaning? We cast a 'spell' with words – and we have to arrange letters in a specific order to 'spell' words.

I hope that as you read further on you'll discover new and more effective ways to create magical moments by changing the way you normally express yourself in various situations. Your thoughts take shape in your mind with words and you express them externally in the same way. So be aware of keeping a rein on your self-talk and choose your words with laser-like precision to give you the best chance of communicating effectively.

Magic was a big influence on my life. I became interested in it at an early age and it taught me about the 'power of suggestion' – how important words were in creating the illusion of bending reality. I was admitted as one of the youngest-ever members to the world's leading magical society.

As well as an early obsession with movies (aside from the 'magic', how many great 'lines' they have provided us with), music is another great passion for me. Again, it was also words that drew me in. I was always aware of the great power in certain song lyrics. Just a turn of phrase in a song can impact a person's life like no 'self-talk' or advice from another person can. I remember the Oscar-winning lyricist Don Black saying in an interview: 'There's something a song can do, that words can't do.'

Compelling lyrics can give us important life lessons. They can inspire you to fulfil your dreams, lift your mood up, get you through sad and difficult times and understand your own deficiencies.

They are words that – thanks to the songwriting skills of the lyricists – help us to understand life better, to make more meaning of life. Songs can evoke feelings and emotions like no other medium. We also associate some songs with certain times in our life, whether it was a time of sadness or joy.

It sometimes takes the pen of the songwriter to put in words what we feel but seem unable to say. Some song lyrics are sheer poetry. I'm often left thinking: why can't we express these sentiments in our communication with others in daily life? Ever heard anybody say 'pride can hurt you too . . .?' Instead of hearing the words 'you don't love me anymore' songwriter Don Black says: 'I'd love to have heard someone tell his girlfriend, "You've lost that loving feeling," on a bus.'

I haven't set out to do a 'painting-by-numbers' book on improving your talk. As always, you can tweak suggested examples to suit your own personality and the situation, while adhering to the *principles*. I remember a surgeon talking about operating on his patients and the necessity of improvisation: 'Of course, you need to know what's in the books in order to do the right thing', he said. 'But if you're limited by thinking in straight lines, you'll never find the solutions. I never think in straight lines.'

We all get entrenched in bad communication habits – with a husband, wife, partner, friend, boss, work colleague or client. It seems as though you can conduct relationships now without ever hearing a person's voice. Face-to-face talk is becoming less of an activity due to electronic devices and email. Even the telephone seems to be shunned, in many cases, in favour of text and email. There's a time and a place for the use of both of those. Communication is instant but it has become *impersonal*.

When you start becoming more mindful of your talk and craft your words with sensitivity, you'll create more of those magical moments and you'll marvel at how a change of words can so affect an outcome. And you won't forget the feeling.

So try out some of the suggestions in these pages and, as the line from the song in *Sunset Boulevard* goes, you'll 'feel the magic in the making'.

2

'iContact' or eye contact?

'Electric communication will never be a substitute for the face of someone who with their soul encourages another person to be brave and true.'

Charles Dickens, *The Wreck of the Golden Mary*

No need to rub your eyes. Yes, these are the prophetic words of Charles Dickens, the great man himself, who had an instinct over 150 years ago – and the telephone hadn't even been invented at the time of his musings.

He was referring, through one of his literary characters, to communication via electric telegraph on a ship during a time of danger. It reflects his scepticism, and how he felt we should converse for important things. (What would he have made of email and social media?)

How often do we come across the term 'eye contact' and its importance? Yet far from becoming more adept, most people seem to have replaced 'eye contact' with 'iContact'.

In most of our interactions there is no question that it is eye contact that facilitates a connection with others and strengthens relationships. (Remember the phrase: 'we see eye to eye on this'?) Think of babies from around the age of six months or so and how they will look to a parent's eyes to pick up meaning.

Communicating with others by computer, iPhone or iPad or other mobile devices is the favoured method for many of us now – let the device do the talking!

Even when present with other people, talking and listening while gazing down at these smartphones and devices is becoming normal. We seem to have crossed the etiquette line as to when it's appropriate to use them – out to dinner, on a date, in a meeting, paying at the supermarket checkout – you name it. What about connecting with people?

Have you noticed that when people are alone, or even with others, as soon as there is a gap in conversation, many of them will reach for their phone?

When speaking face-to-face we gauge the listener's sincerity and interest partly by looking to see where their eyes are focused. Recall how irritating and insulting it is when you see someone looking over your shoulder, or around the room, or at their mobile phone while you are talking.

Continued research shows that it is the positive perceptions that are created by people with good eye contact that makes it so worthwhile to cultivate as a skill (if it's not there already). You come across as more likeable, trustworthy, attractive, confident and powerful – the list of positives goes on (see #10). And, of course, it suggests you're paying attention!

It's our eyes that display an enormous amount of information about what we are thinking at any moment in time. Our body language displays a lot about what we are feeling, and while often we are able to hide true feelings and discomfort with our facial expressions and other non-verbal communication, *our eyes invariably reveal the truth.*

The subject of poor etiquette with mobile technology behaviour is constantly coming up. Research surveys show that there is an element of double standards as to what is considered appropriate phone 'behaviour' in social settings. It appears that upwards of 80 per cent of people believe that using their phones or other devices during a conversation *hurts* the conversation, but that they find it difficult to disengage. Some admitted they deliberately use their phone to cut themselves off from their interactions.

It seems that some of us can't go into a restaurant or coffee shop unless it has Wi-Fi. The new behaviour is to haul out the tablet, phone or laptop and sit there – silently laughing with people we've never met!

Parents, teachers and employers are increasingly worried that young people don't know enough about personal interactions and how to actually look someone in the eye. Is it any wonder, when most of their social maturing comes from behind a keyboard?

Leading academics interviewing primary head teachers in 2015 were told: 'More children are presenting with serious difficulties when it comes to speech and language . . . children's ability to talk, to play, to interact.' As to whether the situation was getting worse, they all agreed and blamed smartphones and the fact that schools are left to address the 'learning gap', when it should be parents engaging more with their children. 'Nursery rhymes and fairy tales might be less interesting than Instagram, but a child's long-term success can depend on them.'

Some people rely on technology as a means of avoiding the personal discomfort of a live, face-to-face (or even telephone) conversation.

Sherry Turkle of the Massachusetts Institute of Technology (MIT) has spent many decades researching people and their relationships with technology. More recently she has been looking at how rapidly advancing technology is having adverse effects on human behaviour. She says: '*Texting and email and posting let us present the self we want to be. This means we can edit. And if we wish to, we can delete. Human relationships are rich: they're messy and demanding . . . the move is from conversation to connection. Worse, it seems that over time we stop caring, we forget that there is a difference.'*

Talking in 2012 to *Time* magazine (in the article entitled 'We never talk anymore'), Turkle said that although adults are less likely to be '*conversation-phobic*', they do become '*conversation-avoidant*'. '*The main reason being because it's easier.*'

Of course, it's the impact on young people that much of the research on texting has focused on. They are at an age where interpersonal skills need to be practised in readiness for their maturity in the outside world. Whereas most adults will have had the advantage of recognising face-to-face communications as the 'norm' before technology came along and handed them a mobile device, concern lies instead with youngsters.

However, Turkle notes that even with adults it's become apparent that there has been an erosion in their competence of having face-to-face conversations since the electronic explosion.

Texting a friend means not having to ask, 'How are you?' and, even worse, getting an answer! '*Too much texting*', she laments, '*means a life of "hiding in plain sight"*'.

Texting and emails have their place in work and personal situations. It's the misuse of them – when talking in person or on the phone may be more appropriate – that's the problem.

The scope for misunderstanding and causing offence is huge, especially as these messages are written with the emphasis on brevity. With a telephone call these misunderstandings don't occur as much and, when they do, they can be addressed there and then.

Be aware of which method of communication to use. Which one will further the relationship?

'3'

'I know you believe you understand . . .'

'I know you believe you understand what you think I said, but I'm not sure that what you think you heard, is what I meant.'

Unknown

There can't be a person in the world who has not said something only to later find that the listener has completely misunderstood what they said – or that they never heard it in the first place There are two elements in our interaction with other people: the *sender* and the *receiver.*

The sender (or speaker) has the job of 'encoding' a message to contain the *right* words, said in the *right* way to make the meaning clear. In addition they have to make sure there is 'congruency' in their body language – so that it doesn't conflict with the message – in order to be credible.

If the words are unclear because they are not part of the 'audience's' vocabulary (jargon, for example) or do not include context that can shape the meaning of words, then problems can occur. Or some words may spark an *emotional* reaction of defensiveness or anger, even though it was not what was meant. That breaks down the listening process.

The receiver (or listener) also has a tough task when you think about it. Their job is 'decoding' the message. Good communication starts with good listening. So, first of all, to even process the information from the 'sender' *they have to pay attention.*

We all know how tough that is; our own thoughts often lead us astray (if we're not mindful in the moment) and so we may fail to hear what is actually said. We have to interpret the message from the sender, paying attention to both the verbal (the words) and the non-verbal aspects of speech (the *way* the words are said – known as 'paralanguage') – as well as observing their body language, if it's said in person.

This interpreting is fraught with difficulty, as words and non-verbal behaviour mean different things to different people, so there is huge scope for misinterpretation at this stage. You have to paraphrase back to the speaker what *you think you've heard* – and to show them that you understand the *meaning* – and not that you've just heard the words. The purpose of paraphrasing is to show the 'sender' that you fully understand the meaning of their message to you. For that reason, be careful that you're doing this and not just 'parroting' back their words.

The difference is enormous. By paraphrasing their views, you give the speaker a chance to reflect on what they've just said, which also gives them an opportunity to reflect on the way the message has been interpreted by you to make sure that *what you heard was what they meant.*

When we think of a conversation we tend to think of talking. But just take a moment and think back to a time when you saw (or heard on the radio) two people trying to talk at the *same* time. It doesn't work. It brings home the fact that the 'listener' is important too.

So be aware that the secret of successful talk is *what* you say, *how* you say it and how well the other person *hears* what you say!

Paralinguistics

(it's the 'melody' as well as the 'lyrics')

'And those who were seen dancing were thought to be insane by those who could not hear the music.'

Friedrich Nietzsche

Scientists at University College London have been looking into solving one of the great mysteries of speech: the way that we as humans are capable of imparting and perceiving information not only with words but also by observing intonation and rhythm.

There's nothing else like human speech in nature – as well as the information carried by the words, you can tell someone's mood, their gender, their age and where they may come from.

The neurobiologists at UCL, using fMRI brain-scanning techniques, have shown how the brain takes speech and divides it into its two constituent parts – words and 'melody' (the varying intonation of speech that reveals mood, gender and other factors).

The studies suggest that words are processed on the left temporal lobe, used for processing, and the melody goes to the right side of the brain to the region that is stimulated by music.

The paralanguage is the *music* or the *melody* accompanying the words that you say. As such it indicates feelings about the message being delivered. It accounts for nearly 40 per cent of the meaning of your message, research studies suggest. It means that when we're decoding feelings, we rely more heavily on the delivery style than the content.

So when we talk about 'paralinguistics' we're referring to the elements of speech apart from the words themselves; in other words(!), the non-semantic aspects relating to the spoken word.

Are you aware of your own paralanguage? How do people perceive your vocal characteristics? Your *volume, pitch, pace* and *intonation*?

- Volume – a loud voice can be seen as dominating. But people who speak too softly can be seen as insecure/shy/lacking in confidence. Changing your voice volume so that it is appropriate for the situation is one of the easier paralanguage elements to alter.
- Pitch is also important. It relates to how high or low you speak. Lower pitches give the impression of being more masculine, authoritative and confident, while higher pitches are associated with being more feminine, caring and friendly. A pitch that's too high can give the impression of someone who is young, inexperienced, nervous or insecure. The voice is very receptive to our emotions and feelings

because of the physiological activity within the body. For example, as well as perhaps an increase in the pace of your speech there may be a tightening of the larynx when in a tense or nervous situation. This produces a voice that has a *higher* pitch.

- Intonation – the way you choose to use melody in your speech. Fluent, comfortable speech has a sing-song element to it that makes it easy and interesting to listen to – ups and downs in tone not only add emphasis to your message but make you sound friendly, approachable, interesting and entertaining. People who speak in monotone are boring. If you sound boring, most people assume you *are* boring!

- Pace – the speed at which you speak has a big effect on your clarity but also on how your voice sounds. Usually, the faster you speak, the higher the pitch becomes. You can come across as sounding anxious, nervous or stressed.

Speeding up speech is a natural reaction to nervous and anxious feelings – the sooner you get all the words out the sooner you can end this terrible experience you're going through (sitting in the interview room with this awful interviewer/blind date/public-speaking engagement).

The opposite end of the scale has its problems too: if you speak too *slowly* you can come across as boring, uneducated and incompetent. It can make the conversation become monotonous and, as far as the listener is concerned, provide more time for their thoughts to wander.

You've heard it said before: it's not just what you say but how you say it. Vocal experts point out that few emotions can escape 'leakage' from the voice.

Try something – say the following phrase in different tones:

'*You want me to go?*'

I've put bold type on the word that you need to stress as you say it:

- '**You** want me to go?'
- 'You **want** me to go?'
- 'You want **me** to go?'
- 'You want me to **go**?'

(Did you pick up on the four possible different meanings?)

The human voice is very closely linked with emotions, and so breathing patterns change when under stress. The muscles become tense and prevent lungs working at full capacity because over-breathing occurs when we're under pressure. So we're still inhaling a lot of air but, since we're breathing fast, there is not enough time to exhale and relax.

You know how, from time to time, you see an actor who gets the voice just *right* for a particular role and you're completely transfixed because the words take on meaning. I remember reading a description of actress Judi Dench's performance in a film:

> '. . . *she unfailingly inhabits a role, leaving you certain no one else would have even touched the sides.*'

So, since 'how we say it' is so crucial in our interactions, then tone becomes the most important vocal quality. The reason for this is that it gives the signal of our attitude at that moment in time.

You've only got to think of the voices that you find easy and interesting to listen to in everyday personal and professional life. What is it about the radio presenters and guests that you find appealing? What elements of the paralanguage would you like to emulate?

Remember that your voice and how you say things has the power to motivate, persuade, charm, command attention and inspire trust. At the other end of the scale it has the power to distort your message and convey the wrong impression.

Be aware of what you can do to make sure 'how you say it' gives the *right* impression.

The 'rhythm' of talking
and listening

'Listen and silent are spelled with the same letters.'

Anonymous

Think about conversations you may have had in which you felt there was a problem with balance. This could be that one person is doing all the talking while the other person assumes, almost totally, the listening role.

This can happen in certain circumstances – when it's called for – but generally the rhythm of an interaction involves both sides being aware of when to speak and when to listen. It works when a rapport has been established. We have to be silent in our speech and especially in our thoughts to fully understand and respond to what others are saying to us.

When you ask people to recall an enjoyable or productive conversation from their personal or working life you'll invariably come across the same rapport-building elements:

- **Encouragers:** In order to show respect and that we are actually listening, we should use certain words at appropriate times. And they have to be genuine. This has the effect of encouraging the speaker to feel more relaxed and carry on. What kind of words? Think of the range of words people use when they're in conversation with you. What about when you're listening? The words are probably similar to these: 'Oh, really', 'Right', 'Go on' and 'Then what happened?' Use these words sparingly and intersperse them during a conversation. It's important to note that you're not implying that you agree with a certain point during their talk (or the opposite), just that you are courteously giving *attention* and following what they are saying. You're displaying empathy.

- **Non-verbal signals:** These include paying full attention with appropriate eye contact and 'listening with the eyes' – the eyes are the most expressive part of our face and we can signal interest and pleasure with our eye movements. Nodding and smiling at appropriate times registers your understanding and indicates that you want the person to carry on speaking.

- **Awareness of 'turn-taking':** This involves avoiding interrupting or changing the subject before the person has finished their point. You've only got to think of your feelings when you are interrupted or when someone changes the subject when you are speaking – you feel that the other person was not interested and can't wait for their turn to speak.

- **Paralinguistic style** relating to tone and delivery also determines the easy flow of the conversation, as well as general body language signals – as noted above. For example, have you noticed how some people lift their chin too high while they're talking or listening to the other person? This sometimes gives the impression of being condescending to the person or their message – even if it's not intentional. What about eye gaze? Is the right amount being exhibited by the listener and the speaker so as to inspire trust and to know that both are engaged in the conversation?

Consider the following:

X: 'So the doctor sent me to the annexe of the hospital. You know, the new building just by A&E.'

Y: 'Right.'

X: 'I saw the orthopaedics chap there and he was really pleased with my progress and said he'd never seen healing that quickly.'

Y: 'Oh, really' (said while looking down at her handbag and delivered with a downward intonation).

X feels as though she's boring Y and feels uncomfortable and wants to bring the conversation to a halt. (She'd like to say to Y: 'You don't give a damn do you . . . ?')

If Y had looked at her, with good eye contact and an enthusiastic smile, and remarked: '*Oh, really*', with an upward inflection, the conversation would have carried on, as Y was displaying empathy. (This encourages more turn-taking in the 'rhythm' of speaker and listener.)

It's often tempting to enquire of someone '*I hope I'm not boring you?*' – you may think you're being empathetic. Well, for a start, you're unlikely to get a true answer. There's also the danger of transferring some guilt over to the other person, as they will think that their body language cues are giving a *signal* that they're uninterested and can't wait for you to finish.

The psycholinguistic element may then come into play through 'suggestion' – having heard the word *boring* it can promote the idea in the listener's mind that your story is less than exhilarating. It's up to the speaker to observe facial expressions and other non-verbal cues to get an idea of the listener's state of mind and receptiveness.

If you see a smile that looks like it has had an overdose of Botox or the eyes are wandering, you can be sure that it may be time to switch topic. If you're doing most of the talking and not asking any questions then yes, you're probably boring them. Time to bring them back into the conversation. Time to listen.

Someone once described it to me in this way:

'We regard speaking as the lead singer of the band. Listening is the bass player – not as glamorous, mostly overlooked, but nonetheless vital for the rhythm.'

It's the 'beginnings' and 'endings'

(the 'primacy' and 'recency' effect)

A re you aware of the primacy–recency effect? It serves you well in all aspects of your life, whether you're speaking one to one, talking to a group, or giving any kind of presentation where you want people to retain important information.

Put simply, the primacy effect states that we remember best the *first* item of information that's presented to us. We remember second best the information that comes *last* – the recency effect. The information that comes in the middle is the least remembered of all.

The psychologist Herman Ebbinghaus (1850–1909) noticed this effect while specialising in memory research. The recency effect describes the increased recall of the most recent information because it is still in the short-term memory. The primacy effect causes better memory of the first items in a list due to increased rehearsal and commitment to long-term memory.

Later scientific studies in memory go on to explain the reason for this retention. The first items of information are processed in working memory and so have a good chance of being transferred to semantic memory. By the time we get to the end of our interaction or interlude the working memory has done its job of allocating the 'data'. It is then free for the arrival of more information to process at the end and therefore retain in our immediate memory. This is the reason we remember 'beginnings' and 'endings'.

An interesting study was done by Solomon E. Asch (*Journal of Abnormal Psychology,* 1946) to test how the impact on the position of words affected our perception of people. In this study Asch used adjectives to describe a person:

- Steve is smart, diligent, critical, impulsive and jealous.
- Steve is jealous, impulsive, critical, diligent and smart.

Who would you find more pleasing to deal with?

Two groups of volunteers were given this information. The first group was given the first statement, the other group the second statement. The first group rated 'Steve' positively and the second group rated 'Steve' negatively.

Can you see why people are apt to remember *first impressions* about people; and also why your exit (see #35) from a situation is also important? When making a decision of any sort, people are apt to remember these things.

What can we learn from this? Be sure that most vital messages are delivered in your *introduction,* and even more so in the *conclusion* of your talk.

PART TWO

Saying it right

'Working from home?
You're a train driver!'

'I said something wrong'

('now I long for . . .')

It's considered that a person's childhood experiences often contribute to their style of communication in later life. If you were raised in a family where talking was like debating, then your linguistic style may be different to someone who grew up in an atmosphere where talk was more about describing experiences, etc.

Words are stimuli – therefore they provoke a reaction or response.

Words use us as much as we use words. In the way that our choice of words is determined by the thoughts that we wish to convey, so also is the way that we *feel* about things responsible for the word choice we make, to express ourselves about these things.

Words that mean the same thing can be used according to whether there is a positive or negative feeling about the topic or person in question. There's a well-known paradigm that illustrates this point:

- I am strong-minded.
- You are obstinate.
- He is pig-headed.

Is it any wonder that so much conflict and tension occurs in everyday speech when emotionally charged words are thrown around like confetti? Simple acts of self-awareness and mindfulness, and pausing before blurting out statements, can preserve relationships. In the example above, referring to a person as 'strong-minded' as opposed to 'pig-headed' may completely alter the response and the course of a conversation.

Do you remember the childhood rhyme: *'Sticks and stones may break my bones, but words will never hurt me.'*? Well, it may have helped us a little in childhood, but is it true? Words can wound and words can heal. And we don't tend to forget hurtful words. I like the following verse:

Sticks and stones may break my bones,
But words can also hurt me.
Stones and sticks break only skin,
While words are ghosts that haunt me.
Pain from words has left its scar
On mind and heart that's tender.
Cuts and bruises now have healed;
It's words that I remember.

Words have tremendous power, and the effect of negative words and statements inflicted against another, be it a child, friend, husband, wife, partner or work colleague, can last from childhood through to a lifetime. As the verse above suggests, the 'bruises' may heal but it's the effect on the psyche and a person's self-esteem that is damaging.

It's a strange thing with words. Just think how long it takes to form relationships and how many words may have passed between your lips during that process.

Yet, the lasting damage of ill-thought-out remarks or responses occurs in the blink of an eye. Sometimes it can just be an innocent turn of phrase that does the damage.

So the words we speak have tremendous energy. They create things, for good or bad. We ruin relationships and marriages because we don't choose our words and/or tone carefully. Then, once the words are out, we realise that in our frustration we've blurted out the wrong words and that things are going to go downhill:

'That's not what I meant to say Lynn – that you don't care.'

'What then? What did you mean? How dare you say I don't care? Do you realise how much time I've spent . . . ?'

All you want to do is 'rewind' the situation and start again. But it's too late. How you long for 'yesterday'.

This happens in our personal and working life all the time. Thankfully, on many occasions we try and rectify things straight after:

'Look Lynn, I meant to say I thought you'd be more careful after what happened last time. Of course you *care* – that's silly. I didn't mean it like that.'

There's the temptation, after we realise we've come out with hurtful words in a situation – and are still in a state of tension – to chastise ourselves for saying something wrong and just leave it. The time to sort out the problem is right there and then, and not to let things fester. In the example above, in a personal life situation, you can be more informal of course. In a more formal or work situation you might approach it in this way:

'Can I just rephrase that – those are not the words I meant to use.'

'I've explained that badly. Please let me make my point differently and hopefully clearer.'

'Sorry, listening to your response – you feel my words were too *strong* in describing Alex's deficiencies. What I meant was that . . .'

Jennifer Graham and a team of researchers at Pennsylvania State University found that using the right words thoughtfully not only has a better chance of ending a conflict but also reduces a health hazard for couples. They found a 'physiological marker' that shows how words can have a significant impact on our health. '*We wanted to know if couples who use thoughtfulness and reasoning in the midst of a fight incur potential health benefits.*'

During a stressful situation, proteins called cytokines normally go up, and this impairs the immune system. 'Typically, if you bring people to a lab and put them under stress, either by engaging them in a conflict or giving them a public-speaking task, you can see an increase in proinflammatory cytokines . . .' Graham said.

By analysing the data she found that words can make a lot of difference in how *high* these proteins rise. In choosing words that reflect thoughtfulness, rationality or caring, the blood tests showed a reduction in the increase of these proteins. The person who used words that revealed he or she was thinking on a deep level – which the study called 'cognitive processing' – attenuated the rise in cytokines every time.

We've known for a while from psychoneuroimmunology (no that's not a typo!) that the body and mind work together. Our thoughts are electrochemical and initiate physical changes in us. What makes words powerful is their ability to change our molecular structure.

There's no doubt that it's far harder to take back our words when damage has already been inflicted. Better to be more aware, when possible, of the 'taste' of your words so that you don't say things you'll later regret.

We should heed this advice:

'*I stop and taste my words, before I let them pass my teeth.*'

Anon

Turn 'closed' questions into 'open' ones

It's amazing how many of us are oblivious to the way that we typically ask questions, often inviting 'closed' responses that elicit either a plain 'yes' or 'no' or a one-word or short answer. You know the kind of thing I mean, don't you? (There you are – I'm at it myself!)

Result: gives the wrong impression, with lost opportunities in many cases.

I was in a hotel bar recently, perched on a stool, overhearing this conversation next to me between a couple of conference-room 'escapees' (John and Alison, their name badges informed me) during their coffee break:

JOHN: 'What kind of work do you do then Alison?'

ALISON: 'Secretarial.'

JOHN: 'Oh, right. Who do you work for?'

ALISON: 'British Airways.'

JOHN: 'How long have you been there?'

ALISON: 'Nine and a half years now.'

JOHN: 'You must like working there, I guess?'

ALISON: 'It's OK.'

JOHN: 'D'you get cheap staff flights?'

ALISON: 'Yes.'

JOHN: 'Where have you been lately?'

ALISON: 'Brighton.'

JOHN: 'Brighton? Ha. Where did you stay?'

ALISON: 'Over at The Waterfront Hotel.'

JOHN: 'Oh, I know. On the seafront, with an atrium? Nice views I imagine?'

ALISON: 'Really nice.'

Where was this conversation going? Absolutely nowhere. John made his excuses and left shortly afterwards, 'safety valve' of mobile phone in hand.

Now, if you were in this situation you may think that Alison's not a very good conversationalist and then start looking for the exit door (as the other person – John – eventually did!). Or you might pause to reflect on the *type* of questions you were asking.

Could there be a better way of getting Alison to open up and share more about herself? It could be that she's a little shy or not the talkative type when first meeting strangers.

The problem with the questions that she was being asked was that they were all 'closed'. The first three or four questions are necessary – of course – to get basic background information. Closed questions elicit short and often single-word answers – quite often 'yes' or 'no'. In addition, even if that's not your intention, you can sound intrusive and intimidating with such questions.

John could have changed tack and allowed Alison to open up by asking her some 'open' questions after the initial background information was out of the way. The bartender *did* – when he began a conversation with her a couple of minutes later – while he was polishing wine glasses:

BARTENDER: 'Forgive me. Couldn't help overhearing. I've travelled on your airline a lot and I used to know some cabin crew that worked there a while ago. You must have seen some changes over the years. What keeps you there year after year?

ALISON: 'I suppose the people I work with. They're really nice – also a great boss, Mr Quarrell. When I talk to some of my friends, they really have problems with people they work with in their organisations.'

BARTENDER: 'That helps a lot – having a good manager. What's the most challenging part of the job from day to day?'

ALISON: 'The stress of deadlines – my boss Simon travels a lot, so he often needs reports prepared quickly. But then, on the other hand, when he's away the workload decreases. So it's fine, I suppose. It balances out.'

BARTENDER: 'You wouldn't happen to know somebody called Mr Grange? I think he's something to do with HR – stays here before a trip, from time to time. I've got to know him well. He advised me about a trip to Montreal to see my son.'

ALISON: 'Mr Grange? He's in my department. I'm a secretary in human resources. Michael looks after events. Well, well – small world. Tell me about Montreal.'

BARTENDER: 'Would you like another cappuccino?' (A 'closed' question – but that was OK!)

The moral is, if someone is shy or initially hesitant it doesn't mean they don't have anything interesting to say. A good conversationalist makes people feel comfortable by asking the right questions. Check your style of questioning.

Open-ended questions, such as those that might start with 'what', 'where', 'when', 'who', 'how' and statements such as 'I'd like to know more about . . .', encourage people to give answers – and add momentum to a conversation. You're giving people an opportunity to share their experiences and feelings, which allows you to find out – often by accident – that you may have things in common. Great for building rapport.

9

Gossip talk

'If you haven't anything nice to say about anybody, come sit next to me.'

Alice Roosevelt Longworth

Few of us can deny that we engage in gossip talk. Sometimes it's framed as 'passing on information' about other people; and then other people 'pass on information' about us.

We're all familiar with celebrity gossip, and the sheer number of magazines and television programmes devoted to the subject shows our insatiable desire to know about the lives of other people. When it's the rich and famous under scrutiny it enables us to pass judgement on them from a distance: 'He may be mega-rich and famous but look at him . . . he's unhappy so he keeps getting caught doing . . .'.

The thing about gossip is that its subject matter is people. The origin of the word is intriguing as it derives from the Old English word *godsibb*, meaning 'someone close to God' and referring to a woman's close female friends at the birth of a child (they become 'godparents').

Later the word evolved to indicate the action of 'talking about the affairs of others'. It's a way for us to bond with people. For some, the purveying of 'information' to others gives them a sense of feeling powerful, when there is no other way of them achieving a sense of power. If it's harmless, there isn't a problem. It's when it's adverse information that is vague or described with innuendoes that problems arise. It's best to be firm and polite in expressing a wish not to hear unsubstantiated claims: 'I'm not quite sure what you mean when you say he's "getting the push" – I'd rather not hear about this until there's more information.' You don't want to be part of the scene and therefore guilty by association. Alternatively, if there is vagueness and innuendoes then challenge the person to be more specific – this often stops them from broadcasting more unsubstantiated claims and rumours.

Robin Dunbar (University of Oxford), who has researched the topic intensively, estimates that about *two thirds* of human conversation is gossip. Other studies go further and analyse how much of this is malicious or disparaging gossip, and it's estimated that the figure is only around 5 per cent.

A recent study in 2012 from University of California, Berkeley (entitled 'Gossip is Good For You') focused on the 'positive' sides of gossip – passing on useful information about untrustworthy or dishonest people:

> '*A central reason for engaging in gossip was to help others out – more so than just to talk trash about the selfish individual . . . when we observe someone behave in an immoral way, we get frustrated . . . Spreading information about the person whom they had seen behave badly tended to make people feel better . . .*'

In the working world, gossip helps us to keep relationships in good order and share common information that affects us. The bad side of gossip relates to the *intention* of the exchange. If it's negative or hurtful information that would be distasteful if it was concerning you and you wouldn't want it broadcast, it's not a good idea to pass it on.

If you have cause to confront someone about spreading rumours or gossip then try to make it non-confrontational. Their motives may be innocent. Since the word 'gossip' is one of those trigger words that invites defensiveness, it's best not to use this word.

What one person regards as 'gossip' is merely 'providing information' in another person's view. So resist saying something like: 'I understand you've been spreading some *gossip* that I'm cutting the workforce in the department and only keeping those people that I like working with . . .'. It invites defensiveness from the start and fails to take into account the nature of the comments.

Instead, try something along the lines of: 'There's a feeling that our department is going to be cut in the near future and that I'm going to be selective about who stays. Rest assured – and I don't mind you passing this on to others – that the headcount will remain the same and we may just merge with another section and have a different name.'

At times when you're unsure of the source of information, then giving an explanation or a denial of something may be counter-productive because of the attention it may attract.

Gossip can be harmless and 'informational', but remember that if it relates to people then it is closely allied to reputation, which is founded on three major principles:

1. What you say
2. What you do
3. What others say about you.

Make sure that you're mindful of the first two principles and be alert to the third!

Rules of eye contact

We hear a lot about eye contact. Some people hit the 'sweet spot'; others seem to have difficulty in understanding the 'rules'. Too much of it can make people uncomfortable, both in personal and professional life, and certainly when seeking romance! An important point that shouldn't be forgotten is that your eyes play a big part in face-to-face communication. It is the strongest of your non-verbal gestures.

It plays a big part every day in your family life, work interactions, business presentations and romantic escapades. You name it . . .

When you or the other person avoids eye contact during an interaction it can make both speaker and listener feel uncomfortable and can also convey the impression of being disinterested and/or dishonest, or just simply bored with the conversation. So apart from regulating the flow of a conversation it gives an indicator to the speaker as to how serious and attentive you are to their message.

Rules of eye contact vary in some cultures. Generally, in Europe, North America and Australia/New Zealand eye contact is associated with trust. Looking away all the time, either while speaking or listening, can signal a lack of interest for whatever reason.

When you make direct eye contact with someone it conveys to them that you are listening. It's perfectly normal to look away to the side, up and down while talking to others. Eye contact should be intermittent. Equally, we can avert our gaze from the other person's eyes slightly, to the rest of their face. The important thing is that it should seem, and be, natural.

Studies have been conducted looking at interactions between a more dominant person and a 'subordinate'. The findings show that the dominant person, when *speaking,* cuts off their gaze more than the subordinate. It appears that the reason for this is that they don't need to 'read' the other person's body language. They're not concerned with knowing their feelings about the message being delivered.

In addition, people who consider themselves to be of high status are inclined to display more direct gaze when talking to others; and those who consider themselves to be of a lower status engage in less eye contact and invariably are the first to break the eye-to-eye interaction.

Equally, the studies show that the more superior person – when in the *listening* situation – may look even less at the other person, turning their gaze to all other areas of the environment in which they're conversing.

What do the studies show about people of 'lesser' status (either real or imagined)? How do they behave? The answer is – exactly the *opposite.*

You can see why, when people assess likeability and trust in other people, their experience of eye contact features heavily in their 'gut' decision. We may think that the other person is telling a lie of some sort if they look everywhere except at our eyes while they're talking. It's the perception that counts.

Of course, sometimes when someone is talking to you they may deliberately avert their eyes because they *are* telling an untruth and are conscious that their eyes may reveal their deceit (*'look me in the eye and say to me that you . . .'*). Equally, if someone feels uncomfortable in a situation or generally lacks confidence, they may find it difficult to maintain eye contact whether they're talking or listening.

In the world of health care, surveys in the UK and USA show that a message from a doctor will be taken more positively when there is more eye contact made. A study by Northwestern University School of Medicine (2013) provided data from videotaped recordings in which special attention was paid to non-verbal communication. They also asked each patient to complete questionnaires rating the doctor's empathy, connection with the patient and likeability. The conclusion was that, apart from the length of visit and social touch playing a part in the perception of a doctor's empathy, the amount of *eye contact* made by the doctor was the most important thing for them.

Paul Ekman, an expert who has been studying facial expressions since 1957, says:

> *'In most interactions we have with other people, we seek honesty. In fact, on most of the public opinion polls that have been done, it comes up as the first or second most important criteria in terms of who we're going to have as a friend, the relationships we want with our children, with our partner or our spouse.'*

Generally people tend to avoid a normal level of eye contact with people that they don't like or if they're being evasive. Maintaining a positive gaze at the other person shows a liking and interest in, or – depending on the circumstance – an attraction to that person.

In a group setting (it could be a meeting or more formal public-speaking event) where you're conversing or presenting to a number of people, there can be confusion as to how to dispense eye contact. It's best to hold intermittent eye contact for a few seconds with each of those present, if it's a small, manageable group.

If we're talking, we need to know that the other person is listening to what we are saying. If there's no eye contact, there's no incentive for continuing to speak. We need signals from the other person that they are paying attention. These are usually visual, with the eyes, with possible vocal cues such as 'yes' and 'oh', and may also be accompanied by head nods (see #5).

We subconsciously rely on these signals, and if they're absent we feel as though we should just shut down and stop talking. Have you ever been in a situation with someone and you're getting no attention signals, so in frustration you exclaim something like (depending on whether it's a formal or informal situation) 'Have you heard anything I said?'

I've asked people in workshops to simulate a real conversation with the person sitting next to them and to listen to them but not show any signs of paying attention. I ask the speaker to imagine it's a real, live situation and at what point does the frustration for them set in as they receive minimal eye contact and no other signals. On average it's between 30 and 60 seconds!

It's bad enough that, even with eye contact, we're having to rely on the person being 'present' while they're giving us their attention, visually. We have to hope that they're in a mindful and not mindless state (see #14).

We can detect emotions from the eyes – anger, fear, happiness, surprise and sadness. When we're talking, the facial muscles around our eyes can betray our emotions to the listener as they result in specific expressions.

Former US president Bill Clinton is often mentioned in the context of attention and eye contact. Gillian Anderson (of *The X-Files* and *The Fall*), appearing on the *Late Show with David Letterman,* said that his appeal was his lingering eye contact.

She exchanged a handshake with him while in a line with other female admirers:

> *'We all, mostly women, lined up. And when he gets to you, he takes your hand and makes eye contact.*
>
> *After he leaves and he moves on to the next person, he looks back at you and seals the deal.'*

The actress was so overcome she expected him to call her up and ask her out:

> *'When I got home, I expected to have a message from him, and I didn't. I bet women across America expect it too.'*

11

Small talk leads
to BIG talk

'Get on your toes, keep your wits about you, say goodnight politely when it's over, go home and enjoy your dinner.'

Terry Wogan

What is it about the term 'small talk'? There's nothing 'small' about it. It can lead to big things. The amazing thing about it is that it can take unexpected twists and turns if you let it.

I hear comments like these time and time again: 'I'm not very good at making small talk'; 'I really find it difficult to strike up a conversation with strangers'; 'I don't want to be intrusive so I don't say anything'; and 'I never know how to begin'.

Of course, it's understandable that there can be unease during the initial silence when you meet somebody new. What seems to concern most people is keeping the conversation going *after* the preliminary introductions.

We're exposed to a variety of situations in everyday life, from casual encounters such as sitting in a doctor's waiting room, standing in line at a bank or waiting for a train, to meeting people socially and to more formal gatherings. We also have encounters that are work-related, in which our content and style of speech will be different.

Here's a question for you. Go on and admit something now. Have you ever started off a conversation, with either a stranger or somebody you know, that relates to the weather?

If you've admitted 'yes' – any idea why you chose the weather as an opener? Research surveys merely confirm what we instinctively know: it's a safe topic and we can be sure that we are both living this experience at the *same* time, so we immediately have something in common with the other person.

After that it is *questioning* that is the key to continuing a conversation. In the early stages of a conversation with a stranger you will naturally find out information about the person, you'll respond with information about yourself and then you'll see if there is common ground.

What are the other safe topics that we can engage in to start a conversation with strangers, aside from 'meteorology' and our immediate surroundings?

I suggest to people that they make a point of remembering the mnemonic:

PHONE. It's a handy *aide-mémoire,* which will eventually become second nature to you when you're interacting with strangers or acquaintances. Touch upon the following topics and see how often your small talk turns to 'big talk':

P: conversation relating to **people** – either that you know in common or people in popular culture or the news.

H: talk about **hobbies** that you both engage in and enjoy.

O: conversation relating to your occupation. If you're in a work-related situation then of course this would be a natural opener. If you work in a similar job, or even if they are in something entirely different, there is fertile ground for learning something.

N: what's in the news is an endless source of discussion material. Try and focus on the 'good' in the beginning, as you want the conversation to be energising and optimistic at the start.

E: the topic of education is a good discussion point – your own past education, your children's, and any courses you're currently attending.

Talking about these topics creates rapport, which is something that is generated between people when they find commonality while talking. That's why we love discovering that someone we've just met went to the same school, knows people that we know, likes the same music, shares the same hobby, works in an interesting job, or has children of a similar age.

There's a kind of balance in any conversation of this sort. You're both exchanging information to and fro, and as a conversation develops you may each disclose more 'personal' information. Therefore an element of trust develops and this reinforces the exchange of more information.

This dynamic can break down if one person spends more time listening, because they feel that their life and their opinions are not interesting. Generally, it can be said that the more extroverted type of person (see #44) copes with this better than those who fall more on the introverted scale (see #45), who may have the feeling of not wanting to be there in the first instance.

So one person has contributed too *much* and the other too *little* – because they consider themselves introverted by nature, for example, or through shyness. This doesn't make for a balanced conversation.

Let's just analyse what a typical conversation might sound like when you meet another person:

- You make certain points or observations:

  'More people here today than I thought there would be.'

  'Yes, there are.'

  'I prefer it when it's busy like this.'

  'Yes, I do too.'

  (Now there's an opening to ask a *question*):

  'How do you feel about their idea to change the venue to allow a residential course from next year . . . ?'

- You ask questions:

  'Have you been to this type of event before?'

  'I went to one in Oxford.'

  'Was it held in one of the colleges?'

  'No, a hotel.'

  'What hotel was it?'

  'Oh, The Randolph Hotel.'

  (*Change of tactic to avoid further short answers*):

  'Tell me about the hotel. I'm interested.'

  'It's a classic. Just had a big refurb. Right in the city centre, just opposite that famous museum . . . now, what's it called . . . let me think . . . the Ashmolean.'

  'That could be interesting for our company. Can I ask you if . . . ?'

Of course, when we're meeting new people either at a social function or at a work-related gathering there is no other way to get an exchange going. It's what we do. It's perfectly natural. Be natural! There's no subterfuge.

When you analyse what prevents small talk progressing into a give-and-take conversation, it's that we, or the other person, sometimes make it difficult for the conversation to progress. For example, the way we either ask a question or answer a question – as you saw in the example above and in the exchange below (see if this rings any bells for you):

'Hi. Have you been to a live concert before?'

'No.'

Of course *you* are now familiar with the fact that she'd been asked a '*closed*' question (**see #8**) so it didn't leave anywhere for the conversation to go.

These questions can invite a one-word response and they don't really get us anywhere if we're trying to 'ice-break' or be friendly and sociable. Yet how often do we engage in this kind of conversation, whether we're asking the questions or on the receiving end?

If the other person is awkward with initial small talk and asks a question that begs for just a one-word response, you are in a better position to *take charge* of the situation and keep the conversation going. How? By providing *more* information than a one-word answer. So instead of just a 'no', which leaves the talk going nowhere:

'No. It's a first and I've always wanted to come to one since my sister told me about a Rolling Stones concert she saw here. How about you?'

'The Rolling Stones? She actually managed to get a ticket for . . .?'

Tone down the 'uptalk'

Y ou've noticed the epidemic, I feel sure. Of course if the 'contagion' has affected you, then it may be that you don't notice it in *yourself* or when you're exposed to it. I'm talking about 'uptalk' – ending a statement with an upward inflection.

Result: it sounds like a question.

For most people, being on the receiving end of statements that sound like questions is highly confusing. The speaker sounds as though they're not sure that what they're saying is true. Or that it will be acceptable to you. And it sounds like they're seeking permission to talk to you.

The point is that in ordinary social conversations this way of speaking may be quite harmless – and acceptable. But in more *professional* settings it can give the wrong impression – a lack of assertiveness.

At its extreme it even sounds like they'll change their mind about the statement if it's not acceptable to you! (Reminds me of the Groucho Marx quip: '*I have principles. If you don't like them, I have others.*')

In working situations, when you're talking to colleagues in meetings or externally with clients, it can give the impression of lack of confidence, lack of knowledge and lack of self-awareness. The rising inflection can cause confusion. You make a statement but it sounds like a question. Consequently, whatever message is given may carry far *less* weight than if delivered in a normal tone.

'Good morning all. My name is Eva? It's the first time I've been here?'

Well, looks as though Eva's name is up for grabs, for starters. The intonation suggests she may be willing to change it if the audience doesn't like it! And it sounds as though she's not sure if it's the first time she's been there either.

What started a long time ago with people in their early teens has, through contagion, now spread to adult men and women. Recent research by linguists at the University of California shows that this way of speaking is becoming more frequent in most varieties of English and also among younger men. '*People who speak uptalk are often misunderstood to be insecure, shallow or slightly dim*', say the researchers, who also reassuringly point out that '*this is not necessarily the case.*' It seems that some people use uptalk as a way of conveying politeness or empathy when conversing with others. But it depends on what the other person 'hears'.

So be aware that it may work in informal conversation but in a professional capacity – *it can convey the wrong impression*? (How did that sound to you?!)

'And every conversation,
I can now recall . . .'

Remember in the Charles Aznavour song, where he looks back on his life and concludes that every conversation seemed to have concerned 'me, me' . . . and just nothing else at all?

Have you ever come across this phrase:

'People who aren't interested aren't interesting'?

It's worth committing to memory. You've come across people in all aspects of life who are only interested in talking about themselves. You give them a chance to let you in to the conversation and then (with a nod to Steven Spielberg), 'just when you thought it was safe to go back' into the conversation . . . they start again.

You know the warning signs for the 'shark attack' with this type of person:

HIM: 'How are you?'

HER: 'Things are not going so well. Had food poisoning, felt dreadful for a couple of weeks. I'm worried about Jeremy. He may lose his job after 11 years with . . .'

HIM: I've got to tell you what happened at the weekend, you won't believe this.'

This person is concerned only with 'Me Me Me'. What should be a conversation is often a monologue. Few people can say, hand on heart, that they have never had experience with this type of person. They have no interest in what you have to say; they wish only to have you listen to their words. The responses you get, if you're lucky enough to receive any interjections, prove this point.

If it's an acquaintance and somebody you see infrequently, while unpleasant and frustrating at the time there is an end in sight. It's more complicated if it's a friend or close family member and you want to share sensitive and troubling thoughts with them.

Some people are just unaware that they operate in this way – talking about things that only concern them, with no capacity for reading body-language cues that show that the listener wants to get into the conversation (or perhaps take their own life!).

When you're unfortunate enough to come up against people like this, quite often they are 'narcissists' who like excessive attention and adulation from others. If you just interrupt, it can annoy this type of person. You can't just take the floor and change the topic. They then make it plain from their 'listening' body language that they're not going to listen to you.

You can try to *bridge* to some point that connects with what they have been saying. Do what the experts do – the talk show hosts and interviewers. Wait for your opportunity and bridge to something that *you* would like to talk about. How is this done? *Listen out for a phrase that can lead to your topic.*

For example:

MARY: 'So I said to him, it's the third time that we have waited in for the delivery and each time the delivery man has had to take the fridge freezer back because it was damaged. They're getting their customer services to call us as I'm so annoyed . . .'

YOU ('bridging'): 'Reminds me of another time ten years ago or so when I was waiting in for a delivery. Anyway, I was getting some curtains made and . . .'

Nobody likes to listen to a monologue. Good conversation is about give and take. We like to gain pleasure from other people's talk, but we also appreciate good listeners.

As the Elizabethan poet and statesman Fulke Greville wrote:

'Our companions please us less from the charms we find in their conversation than from those they find in ours.'

14

Mindfulness or
'mindlessness'?

'No matter what you are doing, you're doing it mindfully or mindlessly.'
Ellen Langer

How good is your attention? Do you feel that you are good at listening? It's been said that most of the time we *hear* – occasionally we *listen*.

Back in the late 1970s, Ellen Langer, a professor at Harvard University, was researching the premise that we take for granted the fact that we pay attention and think before exercising a particular behaviour. Her idea was that we are not mindful most of the time – in fact, we are 'mindless'. Most of our behaviour is accomplished without paying attention, she wrote.

Langer carried out a number of studies to prove her point. At the City University of New York (CUNY) library she approached a student at the copy machine, just as he was about to put his coins in.

The point of the experiment was to ask if she could use the machine first – by using three different forms of the question to test their listening behaviour (and deduce when they 'switched off' listening to the words):

1. 'Excuse me, I have five pages. May I use the Xerox machine?' (straight request)
2. 'Excuse me, I have five pages. May I use the Xerox machine because I have to make copies?' (meaningless reason)
3. 'Excuse me, I have five pages. May I use the Xerox machine, because I'm in a rush?' (sentence contains an excuse/explanation)

If people were rational then the results would have shown that we would be more likely to grant the request for those with a *valid* reason or explanation (3). But that's not what the studies showed.

Offering *any* reason – including the meaningless one (2) – led to compliance. There was hardly any difference between (2) and (3). By contrast, (1) had a very low 'yes' rate.

Her analysis suggested that people didn't listen to the entire statement and she inferred that they listened up to the word 'because' and then tuned out and gave an affirmative. So it appears that just giving a reason for an action, especially using the word 'because', is very powerful.

After observing these studies her students carried out the same studies, which provided similar results – a display of 'mindlessness'.

Langer's definition of this state was one in which we resist what comes naturally to us by filling in the blanks *before* we hear or see something.

Langer decided to specialise in the 'study of the antidote', which she referred to as 'mindfulness': a state in which we pay attention and listen – in the moment. Some now dub her as 'the mother of mindfulness'.

We spend a lot of time listening as well as talking. Being 'in the moment' and *hearing* what people are saying can only come about when we're mindful. So be mindful of being *mindful*.

You reveal your *true* level of interest by the way you listen

Ever heard the statement 'The best conversationalists are the ones who are the best listeners'?

You may be familiar with the term 'active listening'. It refers to a state where, after you've 'given the floor' over to the other person to talk, you remain fully present and attuned to the other person's words and emotions.

There's always a temptation to let the mind wander, and in many instances the astute speaker will pick this up while they're speaking to you. Many people are sensitive to attention and may feel offended or frustrated when they sense that they have lost the listener.

It may be the case that you are generally respectful and attentive when listening to other people after you have had your say. Yet there are people – and you may have come across them – who have no idea of how their body language, including a glazed look, is affecting the speaker. They may look as though they're 'present' only when it's their turn to speak – at other times their mind is wandering.

We tend to notice subliminally how people respond to us *physically*; and, what is more, typically we make judgements and decide whether we like them or not on this basis.

An interesting experiment was carried out by psychologists, in which they asked a group of participants to talk about themselves – on harmless topics such as hobbies and interests. A person of the other sex watched and listened to each speaker. They were confederates who were told to vary the amount of gaze, smiles and how much they leaned forward towards the speaker as he or she spoke. The speakers were asked to do an evaluation of the listeners based on a number of dimensions, including how likeable they were.

What were the results of the findings? Predictable, but nonetheless instructive for all of us: the speakers liked the listeners best when they gazed at them, smiled a lot and leaned towards them.

So the moral is: after you've had your say (or even if you're in a situation where you've said *nothing*), when you assume the listener 'role', smiling, gazing and leaning forward will increase your likeability more than if you adopt a neutral body position.

Fight or flight?. . . the 'amygdala hijack'

Neuroscientific studies have been carried out to show the workings of the brain when a person hears a statement that relates to their 'status' or self-image being assessed or challenged. The much talked about 'fight or flight' mechanism is activated and it inevitably puts us in defensive mode.

Daniel Goleman (author of *Emotional Intelligence*) says: '*Emotion makes us pay attention right now . . . it gives us an immediate action plan without having to think twice. Do I eat it, or does it eat me – you don't sit around and Google it.*' The emotional response '*can take over the rest of the brain in a millisecond if threatened*'.

Goleman noted that '*. . . the architecture of the brain gives the amygdala a privileged position as the emotional sentinel, able to hijack the brain*'. He coined the term 'amygdala hijack' for the part of the brain that responds irrationally when threatened. The amygdala is the emotional part of the brain responsible for regulating the fight or flight response. Stress hormones take over, before the prefrontal lobes – which regulate 'executive function' – can mediate the feelings and therefore reactions.

> 'Can we put a meeting in the diary for Friday morning? *I need to discuss something with you urgently.*'
> 'When you're not needed on the shop floor this morning Chantal, could you pop into my office? *Something needs to be sorted out.*'
> 'Sarah. We didn't hear you get in last night – we were up till one o' clock. *We need to talk.*'

With statements like these you feel that the interaction is not going to be a pleasant one. Or rather, it's not going to be delivering good news! With any kind of criticism, whether it's delivered at home, by a friend or in the working environment, *how it is said* and *how it is received* determine its effectiveness.

A headmaster-to-pupil tone is rarely productive. The paralinguistics are important when you're about to give any kind of criticism or assessment. It's especially delicate. You want to minimise the anxious feelings that the message inevitably generates – inducing the fight or flight emotional reactions.

If you're the one delivering these types of statements, if you're able try and give some prior information beforehand when you ask for a talk that's at a later time; or if it's immediate let them know at the beginning. A person's anxiety level (fight/flight) will be determined by your words. Even if it is negative messages you will be imparting, you will get more out of a person if you can reduce their anxiety levels.

So, what would be better in the earlier examples if you had scope to legitimately 'soften' the message?

'Can we get something in the diary for Friday morning? We'll have a chat about how we can get your department to make sure mid-afternoon orders always make the last post pick-up.'

'When they can spare you off the shop floor this morning, Chantal, just pop into the office for a moment. We just need to make sure the codings are going out correctly so that we don't run short on the shelves.'

'Sarah. We didn't hear you get in last night – we were up till one o'clock. We'll talk later – Dad wants to make sure we've got contact numbers other than your mobile, for future occasions.'

The situation is especially difficult when we have to give unfavourable comments relating to a person's character or habits:

'It's been said that you're always so negative, Mark. It's draining to be around you.'

This becomes a personal attack on the person with no emphasis on telling them what they can do to improve the situation. A better choice would be:

'Mark, try and be more upbeat with the newer members of the group. It becomes a bit contagious when they hear our gripes.'

The goal is always to *separate* the person's behaviour (actions) that invites the criticism from you, from the person himself (or herself). That makes it much easier to comment on their behaviour without causing offence.

There are two golden rules when criticising – and this applies to both personal and working-life situations:

1. To gain attention and make the focus on the behaviour you would like to see *changed*. You're not commenting on what the person *is*. Which of the following comments do you think reduces defensiveness and invites more attention?
   'You're messy – the way you work.'
   'Your desk looks messy, Anthony.'

2. Avoid use of statements in the active voice. Aim for statements phrased in the *passive* voice. Compare these two statements:
'You upset Anne with your remarks.'
'Anne felt very upset by your remarks.'

The personal element ('You') is taken away from the statement and redirected to the *cause* ('remarks').

Another way of voicing criticism that invites inner stress and tension is the use of *multiple* questions that, rather than inviting genuine answers, are deployed to make the person feel guilty. It's almost like a multiple-choice questionnaire:

'Did you think that nobody would notice? Or did you assume that the department likes wasting money? Or is it that you thought because of your long service you're immune from scrutiny?'

Since the true reason for phrasing things this way is to highlight a person's deficiencies and not to seek *answers* to the questions, it rarely does anything but promote bad feeling.

It's far better to use a more productive way of making your point and expressing concern, and giving them a chance to explain why they behaved in a certain way:

'Lucy – I'm concerned about budgets. Help me understand why you chose to . . .'

You're still able to respond, if necessary, by showing you can understand why they did/thought something without actually agreeing with them:

'Yes, I can understand why you may have thought that. Let's look at the repercussions that it's caused . . .'

We're all giving and receiving criticism much of the time in various settings. In the workplace it takes on a more structured role when you may be delivering – or on the receiving end of – some formal 'constructive feedback' (see #47); but it's still a case of somebody voicing concerns about another person's behaviour. You need to elicit a response that comes from a position of courtesy and emotional intelligence – and not the 'amygdala hijack'.

'We need to talk'

(warning!)

Come on, cast your mind back. Have you ever said these four words or something similar? Has someone said it to you? Think back to childhood, your parents and your school.

MOTHER: 'When you're back from school later, *we need to talk.*' (Your thoughts: 'I'm grounded – for coming home late two nights in a row'.)

TEACHER: 'Come and see me at the end of the lesson.' (Your thoughts: 'Oh no, extra homework for . . .'.)

This carries on into adulthood – at work and at home. Ask any man or woman how he or she feels when the spouse or partner says: '*We need to talk . . .*'. That sinking feeling in the pit of the stomach. That reflex inner talk ('Oh no. Not now. **Not never!**') Those movies you've seen with one or the other of a couple uttering those words – before 'all hell breaks loose'!

When you utter these words – and research suggests that these words are uttered more by women than men (although by no means exclusively) – then the other person knows that something good is unlikely to follow.

Ever heard a conversation like this?

HER: 'We need to talk.'

HIM: 'Fine, go on. I've got a couple of minutes before I leave for work.'

HER: 'I just wanted to say thanks for cleaning the bath, taking the rubbish out, not leaving your wet towel on the bed and not spilling beer on the rug.'

Doesn't happen does it? When those four words are said, the listener knows:

- that it's *not* going to be about anything positive
- that it's going to be about something that *wasn't* done or was done *incorrectly*
- the conversation is going to involve a lot of *emotion* (great for men!)
- it's certainly going to be something you'd rather *not* discuss.

So, if you want to avoid defensiveness with your partner, consign these words to Room 101. Just come out and say what the problem is. Just talk!

Equally, at work this opener (whether it's a woman addressing a man or woman, or a man addressing a woman or man) should be avoided. These four words are explosive.

Try some alternatives:

'Quick talk? Got time now, or when's good?'

'Just need something explained. Can we do it now?'

Try and avoid 'We need to talk' whenever you can. It will change the course of your conversation by reducing defensiveness at the outset. You don't want to send out a warning. You promote anxiety and invite conflict.

The power of the pause . . .

('go ahead . . . make my day!')

'The notes I handle no better than many pianists. But the pauses between the notes – ah, that is where the art resides.'
                                             Arthur Schnabel, concert pianist

D o you take advantage of the power of the pause to improve the impact of your message? As I once heard someone explain succinctly: your pause gives importance to what *precedes* it and to the message that *follows* it.

It can act as a signal to your listener(s) that an important point follows or allow the listeners some time to take in your previous message. It's very effective if you do it after you've said something that you would like them to retain – a *key* point of your message.

Many speeches or presentations are just statement after statement, bombarding the listeners without giving them any respite for thinking about individual points. Nervous presenters, confronted with the stress of the occasion, are inclined to speak faster and faster and this doesn't allow the audience time to think about important points. If you insert pauses after the messages that you would like the listeners to retain, it helps with their recall. It gives them time to think and reflect on what they've heard.

The pause is also beneficial for you, the speaker, as it gives you an opportunity to relax a little and to get ready for your next statement. It allows for a smooth transition to the next point with more fluency.

Also, as far as your listeners are concerned, if you pause after one point you're also then allowing them a break in attention span in preparation for your *next* point. So if you're delivering a number of important points, if you pause after you've covered one area, you're letting them know that you've finished and a new point is now to be covered.

Pause before the punch line or conclusion as it creates suspense: 'As we pause for reflection here, I'd like to make a key point to you'.

Your pause invariably seems longer *to you than it does to the audience.*

So, be aware that your concern about the length of pause is usually not shared by your audience. Instead, your ability to insert pauses makes you look confident and in control. The pause has power. Use it. *Go ahead . . . make my day!*

Is 'fine' the new 'F-word'?

Perhaps you've noticed it subconsciously when hearing the word said by other people, but you're too busy saying it yourself to consciously register it?

What am I talking about? The word 'fine'.

Somehow the original meaning of the word as an adjective and adverb has been demoted to a catch-all term that we use to describe the different aspects of our life. And quite often it's now used to masquerade our *true* heartfelt feelings. It says nothing:

'How's the job going?' 'Fine.'

'What do you think of the red wine?' 'Yeah, it's fine.'

'Do you mind if I sit here?' 'That's fine.'

'How's your love life Joanna?' 'Fine.'

'Sorry I'm late, I know it's not a nice place to wait.' 'It's OK, it's fine.'

'Fine'. The new four-letter-word response, in its various forms. It's a learned response. Maybe it's because we're conditioned to respond, in this way, to friendly interactions where the initial enquiry is 'how's things?' or 'how are you?' or 'do you need some help with . . . ?'

For all of these you may feel that the response 'fine thanks' or 'no I'm fine' is because that is really all the enquirer's *attention span* or interest level will tolerate. Our feeling is that people are just being polite – *with little concern for our eventual answer* – so we don't answer with total honesty and instead give the short answer.

Of course, there's nothing wrong with the word in its purest form – to indicate that things are agreeable. It's just that the ubiquitous use of the word is usually perceived as a:

- polite way of responding briefly (when our situation is agreeable *or* disagreeable)
- means to cut a conversation short (you don't want to talk about your situation or you feel that the other person would not be interested)
- passive–aggressive response that conceals frustration, anxiety, dissatisfaction or anger.

There's no doubt that in most instances these requests for information on a daily level are more social pleasantries than asking a burning question.

Perhaps we should observe the 'paralinguistics' for a start – how the statement is phrased. And the rest of the 'body talk'. Our own way of communicating may not invite truthful answers so we need to pay attention to the signals that are given.

If the person is hiding behind a defensive 'fine' and we feel that they're not being honest, then it's up to us to challenge it – in the right way.

Not a 'I don't believe you're being honest' type of statement that will invite defensiveness and possibly also anger and frustration, but a more tactful approach along the lines of:

'Ken, I know you said the training of the interns was coming along fine but Fiona tells me you've had to work late three times this week and you've had problems with train times. Let me get Laura to take over late afternoon. It won't be a problem.'

'You said you're fine. I just feel that you're upset about something. I wonder if there's anything I can help you with?'

In close relationships you may follow statements like the preceding one with something that may reflect on your own past behaviour. 'Is it something I said . . . or didn't do?' Of course (if you're lucky!) it may be nothing to do with you. It may be something external that is not related to you or your actions. In which case, you've opened up a dialogue and can help the person by *listening* to their perceived problem and hopefully make them feel better.

So what about the times when things are 'fine' with you – *genuinely*? And you can't break the habit:

'How's things this morning?'

'Fine.'

'Oh, good.'

According to the habitual 'offenders', the trick is to just give more *detail* to avoid misunderstanding.

'How's things this morning?'

'Fine. Trains were on time, Lucy's handed me a report early and I've just had an invitation for lunch.'

'Wow. Have a good day!'

Meaningful conversations are lost and relationships fractured when we take the word at its *face value*. We're all guilty of it. Sometimes it's just easier than giving long explanations, especially when it concerns some on-going situation: a health problem, a business problem or a relationship problem.

So be aware of the use of this word. It can be used to hide true feelings, or because it's just easier to reply with that one word if you don't want to go into detail about something.

Sometimes, as we noted earlier, that's all that people want to hear after the 'how are you?', for example. It just becomes part of the script. Tell somebody about the health problems of your goldfish and see whether 'fine' might have been a better option. You know from a person's response as to whether the short answer would have been better. If they care about the topic they're likely to ask you another question.

We need to adjust our own linguistic style and behaviour and on the flip side, observe the other person's body language and paralanguage. That way, the important points we need to know about (or someone would dearly like to *talk* about) are welcomed and not masked with the 'fine' retort.

20

Invert your 'BUT'

(and we're not talking about a Pilates move!)

We're all guilty of it. We know the effect it has on us when we're on the receiving end. The dreaded single word – 'but'. Yet, despite the demotivating effect it has on us, we carelessly use it when talking to other people. It goes something like this:

'I really enjoyed the theatre, thanks for the tickets – *but* I did think the orchestra was a bit too loud.' *(outing with a friend)*

'I'm very pleased with the work that I've seen, so far, *but* could you make more effort with sticking to the time schedule for each project.' *(meeting with your manager)*

'The last quarter, Q4, produced some great figures with the celebrity biographies *but* we've got a lot of hard work to do if we're to meet this year's targets.' *('motivational' group meeting)*

Well, for most people (sensitive creatures that we are) it conjures up another single word – 'OUCH'!

The word 'but' has the effect of *discounting* all that precedes it. To put it bluntly – it's a downer. It takes away any joy, compliment or good feeling that comes from a statement. More often than not, as well as taking away any motivation or joy that we might have felt, it can also lead to a feeling of *antagonism* towards the speaker. Tragic, if that's not the feeling you wanted to engender. Or, more importantly, the effect *you* wanted to create.

So, play it smart. Invert your 'but' (well, you know what they say, 'no pain, no gain'!). Get your 'but' statement to come *first*. That way the brain processes and remembers the *last* thing that's been said – a *positive* statement. Let's rephrase the statements above:

'The orchestra was a bit on the loud side but I really enjoyed the theatre – thanks for the tickets.'

'We just need to get you up to speed on deadlines but I'm very pleased with the work that I've seen so far.'

'We'll need to work hard for this year's sales but the last quarter, Q4, produced some great figures with the celebrity biographies.'

Be watchful with your speech (and thoughts – remember your 'self-talk' can be highly demotivating) and make a conscious effort to notice how many times you veer towards using the negative 'but'.

Remember that this short but powerful word can rob your statement of any goodwill that you create in the first part of your sentence; defences come up and the listener just waits for the 'post-but' statement. Invert your statement so that the 'positive' element doesn't get lost. It may take time to break the habit, *but* watch the huge difference in outcomes!

'And' another thing . . .
(while we're on the subject)

We have looked at the demotivating value of 'but'. There are some instances when, if it feels more appropriate – and if the statement warrants it – a simple substitution of '*and*' may be suitable.

You may remember that the phrasing of the statements with the positioning of the 'but' meant that the focus was on what needed to be done in the *future*. Sometimes a simple '*and*' can be used instead, which results in separating the two parts of a statement to show that the two points can coexist. Here's an example:

> 'I did go for a really long run today Mum – you can see the blisters – *but* I ate a lot of stodgy food and drank sugary soft drinks after I met Kate in the canteen.'

As it stands, this statement robs her of the joy and power of the acknowledgement to herself: that she had done something to promote her wellbeing. Instead, it focuses on what she didn't like – the knowledge that she'd eaten food and drink that was bad for her.

Even better for her would be a rephrasing of the statement, which would not alarm her parent so much and also lead to less guilt and chastising on her own part; a simple change that would alter the attitude of her listener (her mum) and, more importantly, herself. If you use the word 'and', you're not conveying that there's any 'downside' to your statement or achievement:

> 'I went for a really long run today Mum. **And** I ate some stodgy food and drank sugary drinks with Kate afterwards . . .'

This helps her acknowledge the good thing that she did (the exercise), despite indulging in the treats that she knowingly succumbed to. It's the same statement – but this time with no judgement, which is important as our 'self-talk'(as we discussed earlier) is very powerful.

In the same vein, when you're delivering some kind of feedback to another person:

> 'Well, Tom, you did a great job in organising the contractors for this second-floor refurbishment *and* this time, hopefully, we can pull out the stops for it to actually finish on the scheduled date.'

> 'This report is fine Mandy, *and* we can perhaps just get the pages numbered with those statistics highlighted, as I mentioned, then we can distribute it to the department.'

Sometimes that three-letter word can defuse potential conflicts and bad feeling, if you're alert to it – **and** it just requires a little thought! You're giving feedback to a person in a way that conveys 'you did that well *and* if you do X it could even be better'.

Interject . . . don't *interrupt*

I like this piece from *Esquire Etiquette,* in which it is noted that there are two forms of interrupting:

> *'The obvious one, interrupting the speaker in mid-sentence, is easy to avoid; just wait until the other has stopped talking before you start. (And don't ever say, "Have you finished?". You might as well say right out that he's a windy numskull and you thought he'd never run down.)'*

Fair to say that we've all been subject to this situation, and also been guilty of interrupting others mid-sentence. And we've also experienced and been guilty of the second kind of interruption, as the article goes on to say:

> *'The other kind of interruption, equally culpable, is often prefaced by "That reminds me . . ." or "By the way . . .". Such phrases usually signal a digression or irrelevancy. When you interrupt another's train of thought, or send a discussion off into a tangent, you indicate that you are either stupid or rude, either unable or unwilling to stick with the speaker's point.'*

More than 60 or so years later (yes, this was from the 1954 edition of *Esquire Etiquette*!) these sentiments still hold true and are more important than ever.

Because we think faster than we speak it's always tempting at certain stages to interrupt. Resist. It's distracting for the speaker and prevents you from discovering more information.

You know how you feel when somebody interrupts you while you're in the middle of your talk. It depends how it's done, but in most cases it doesn't leave you with a good feeling. It can spoil a relationship because it can convey the message that you can't be bothered to listen and you don't value their contribution.

The problem is that most people don't take the trouble of learning the *difference* between an interruption and the more acceptable interjection.

When you spoil the flow of somebody's talk by wading in with your own comment, you're interrupting. If it adds no value and just seems like poor manners then the person may be offended (even though they don't voice it). Body language usually gives a good indication of how they feel about it.

If there's a natural gap in the conversation then you can interject with a comment, or a signal of approval. (Just make sure the gap is not the speaker's natural pause just before he's about to make a further point.) Sometimes it's done out of excitement – it can be one word like 'really' or 'oh'. The important thing is that it's done for the right reason.

The difference between interjecting and interrupting is that with the former your idea or statement of agreement or encouragement *enhances* the overall tenor of the discussion. 'You know something, I think that was really brave of you . . . Do carry on.' It's usually *polite*, whereas interrupting doesn't create the same effect with the speaker.

Sometimes, even a well-intended brief interjection can throw the speaker, and they forget what they had previously been saying. So, if possible, try and remember the last words that were being said by him or her. It's always good to do that because it eliminates any embarrassment on the part of the speaker (if they have forgotten) when you say: 'Do carry on – *you were saying that* the research on the radio advertising listening figures is out on . . .'.

Be aware that interrupting at the wrong time can sometimes lead to unintended consequences. Be careful and be mindful. Look what happened here:

A vacuum salesman appeared at the door of an elderly lady's cottage and asked if he could 'come in for a few moments'. Interrupting her protestation of '*No, I need to tell you something . . .*', he rushed into her living room.

'*No, you don't understand they've . . .*' she continued, but was interrupted again as he declared: '*Watch this.*' He then threw a large bag of dirt all over her clean carpet. '*If this new vacuum doesn't pick up every bit of dirt, I'll eat all the dirt.*'

The woman, who had now reached the limit of her patience, replied: '*Sir, if I had enough money to buy that thing, I would have paid my electricity bill before they cut it off this morning. Now what would you prefer, a spoon or a knife and fork?*'

23

Assertion not aggression

'Watson. Come at once if convenient. If inconvenient, come all the same.'
Arthur Conan Doyle, message from Sherlock Holmes to
Dr Watson, *The Adventure of the Creeping Man*

It's a term we repeatedly hear, especially in the workplace, in its various commands: 'Be assertive . . .' or 'Show some assertiveness and . . .'.

The problem is, in the wrong hands it quite often tips into aggressiveness and in many cases it's because people are not quite sure of the difference.

The result: your interaction causes upset or defensiveness or offence and general bad feeling. You may end up getting what you want but at the cost of fractured relationships.

Some people seem to be energised by arguing. Try and avoid them or cut the conversation short if you can. Eventually, the lack of engagement and your grunting and dismissive body language should drain their excessive energy.

A good definition contrasting the two approaches is:

1. assertive – you are concerned about yourself and others
2. aggressive – you are more concerned about yourself than others.

When you're using assertive talk you're making your wants and needs known in a clear, confident and non-offensive way; and in 'sticking up' for yourself you're preserving your 'self-esteem' (there's another ubiquitous term!).

The problem seems to be that those of us whose behaviour could be described as 'passive' find the transition to assertive talk quite difficult at first. We can define passive people as those who don't tend to state their opinions at all.

At the other end of the spectrum there are those who find it difficult to step down from *aggressive* talk to the more productive assertive way of speaking. It's quite uncomfortable to admit to yourself or others that you're passive or aggressive, isn't it?

When you do, it helps you feel more confident and you can communicate more effectively. These are the options:

Assertive – I win, you win
Aggressive – I win, you lose

Look at the jump from a passive to an assertive request to a boss in the following examples:

Passive: 'Can I order a new reception coffee-table machine to . . . err . . . replace that antiquated thing we've got at the moment?'

(This kind of statement can invite a flat refusal because of the way it is phrased.)

Assertive: 'What kind of budget might we be able to allocate for a new reception coffee-table machine, so that visitors don't get a bad first impression on arrival?'

(This is phrased in a more assertive way, with a 'reason' for action, and in a way that doesn't invite a flat rejection – the power of suggestion.)

If you're expressing assertion in the right way, then you're not averse to expressing a difference of opinion in situations. You're also able to show any displeasure or annoyance in a *non-threatening* way.

Remember the big difference that exists between assertion and aggression. Aggressive people may ignore or attack the opinions of others since they're only concerned with their own. The assertive person is able to state their opinions while at the same time being respectful of the views of others.

24

I should avoid 'should'

We'll talk about when we use the word 'should' when talking to someone in a moment, but first a question to you. Have you ever noticed how feeling like you *should* do something evokes a certain amount of tension within you when you're having a conversation with your own inner-self?

The voice tells you: '*You should think about getting a personal trainer.*'; '*You should think about getting another job.*'; 'You should get in touch with Mary, it's getting ridiculous.'

These thoughts are all designed to promote anxiety within you. You fix up a first session with a personal trainer and on the way there you feel a sense of nervousness. Your self-talk then obligingly tells you that you 'should' be excited not nervous. So now we feel we shouldn't be having the feelings that we're experiencing and should be excited. More guilt!

The point is that the word invites resistance and disempowers you. It takes away your autonomy.

You can substitute it for other words such as *might* or *could*:

'I *might* get in touch with Mary at some stage this summer.';
'I *could* look into the job situation over at the new clinic that's opening in June.'; or
'I *could* do 30 minutes of . . .'.

This takes away the pressure and anxiety and mentally puts you in *control*, enabling you to make an assessment. You may say to yourself, 'I could do that, but I feel that 15 minutes is perfectly OK at the moment.'

We've been talking about the word 'should' with our own *inner talk*. What about when we're voicing the words to other people? If it has that effect on us, what does it do when we start 'shoulding' other people? Does it sound condescending, even though you mean well?

'John you really should smarten up your wardrobe.'

'Sophie, you should brush up on how to answer the phone if clients' calls come through directly to this line.'

Maybe the resistance comes from listening to our parents: 'Why do I have to . . . ? 'Because I said you *should*.'

Along with 'should' there are a few other words that invite conflict:

must
need to
ought to
have to

We're all averse to hearing these words. Along with 'should', these words suggest that there is some rule of the universe or some outside body that decrees you have to do these things. Few people like to be told what to do – that they *must/need/ought/have to* do something.

You might consider using '*you might*' . . . and watch the change in the reaction that you get.

25

Never say 'never' again

Have you ever analysed the effects of the word 'never?' And what about other 'absolutes'? But we'll come to those later.

The word 'never' is one of those words designed to get you in trouble – even if there's a degree of truth in it, quite often there's an element of exaggeration that is born out of frustration. Recognise it and try and craft your words to take the accusatory element out of the statement. It is one of those generalisations that causes the listener to react with defensiveness and also attempt to prove you wrong. It often causes friction and anger:

X: 'You're never on time whenever we've got a train to catch.'

Y: 'That's not true. Twice I can remember being on time – at King's Cross earlier this year and a couple of years ago at Euston when we were going to York.'

X: 'We never go out to dinner.'

Y: 'What? We haven't been for the last few months, but you know why. Until this new project is finished in a couple of months' time, I can't get back before nine.'

X: 'I never get reports back from you on the day you state they'll be in.'

Y: 'Well, I admit the last three times there's been a problem with the schedule but last year there were no hitches.'

Possible alternatives to these statements, for a more sympathetic and constructive response, would be:

'Was there a problem on the journey in? We've got four minutes for the train.'

('Yes, I'll tell you later – accident on the Underground. Let's make a dash.')

'When can we look forward to going out to dinner again?'

('Oh, sorry. The project will be ending in six, seven weeks' time – we'll be back to normal then.')

'Is there something going on that's preventing the reports being on time the last few times?'

(She'll likely explain to you that they are one short in the typing section due to a maternity-leave absence).

There are other 'absolutes' that encourage defensiveness and destroy a message. Words such as:

everyone

everybody

no one

always

They – like the 'never' statements – are rarely true. These absolutes invite people to challenge the word itself, instead of the point of the statement.

Equally, people speak in a way that invites challenge:

'The kids of today have no manners.'

'All the politicians are in it for themselves.'

'Cyclists are a menace on London's streets.'

'TV shows such rubbish these days.'

'Mary said foxes always attack babies.'

Of course these statements can easily be challenged with the same response: 'What, *all* of them?'

It's in the nature of human beings to make observations and describe them in a general and lazy fashion that attempts to give validity to our argument. The trouble is, it takes away from our message. Of course, if you're in conversation with someone who's taking a negative view of the world – and remember the saying 'misery loves company' – you might find support for all of these statements!

We could gain support for our ideas and keep our personal reputation intact by perhaps using statements such as these to replace the above:

'A lot of kids today don't seem to have been taught any manners.'

'You get the feeling that many of our politicians are only in the job for themselves.'

'Many cyclists in London make it difficult for themselves . . .'

'A lot of TV programmes these days are just not worth watching.'

'After the attacks on babies by foxes, Mary said it's unsafe to leave babies on their own.'

When we engage in absolutes it invites people to refute the statement outright and so the point of the statement gets thrown away 'with the bathwater'. It's something we all do (ooops!). I'll qualify that: it's something we all do *from time to time*. (That's probably a statement that would not be challenged!)

I remember David Frost was interviewing a politician who said to him: 'Sometimes I think *everyone* in the world hates me.' Quick as a flash, his interviewer replied:

'No, no. You're being hard on yourself. *Everyone* in the world hasn't met you *yet*.'

Don't ask me 'WHY'?

'WHY?'

Have you noticed the destructive nature of this word? The accusatory nature when it's used relating to *people*?

There is probably no other word that encourages *defensiveness* in a person than this small word. Cast your mind back to instances in which you may have used it and what kind of reaction it provoked:

'Why haven't you done this?'

'Why is this late?'

'Why didn't you tell me?'

'Why did you do that?'

'Why do you feel that way?'

'Why would you do such a thing?'

When it is used in an accusing way it can completely *alter* the course of a conversation and provoke a hostile reception from the other person.

The problem with this word is that, apart from sounding accusatory and, at times, aggressive or personal, it requires us to give a *rational* explanation for our behaviour.

When we're asked a 'why' question, in most instances the request is for us to *justify* our behaviour or feeling. The trouble is – irrational beings that we are – we often don't know the reason *why* we behave in a particular way. We're asking our rational brain to make sense of a decision in which it had no involvement! It's often down to gut feeling or intuition.

I once had a manager whom I noticed always handled any conflict or complaint situation about a member of staff (either internally or externally) in a similar way. If somebody had made a blunder, was late with something, had an altercation of some sort, forgot to inform him about something, he handled it in a *non-judgemental* way. He used to use just two words: *what happened*?

The benefit of this (and I know this first hand) was that it encouraged people to open up because it wasn't a blaming question, it was inviting dialogue. The result was that he found out more information – nothing stifles good dialogue more than defensiveness – because it encouraged people to give the background to events.

So, unless it's a situation where you want to put somebody on the spot for whatever reason, try to rephrase your questions.

How constructive are these for example?

'Why did you take that road? The left hand looked more direct.'

'Why can't you be on time for Monday-morning meetings?'

'Why is the car so untidy when we have to give a lift to John's classmate?'

The words used in the following questions would probably generate better dialogue and certainly less friction:

'Do you think the left fork back there would have been any quicker?'

'Is there a reason Monday mornings are difficult for you?'

'We need to make sure the car's tidy if we're giving John's classmate a ride.'

Always remember that, with a little bit of thought, you can elicit the same kind of information without using the provocative *why* word. The bonus? Less bad feeling and the prospect of a conversation rather than defence and altercation.

Don't ask me why!

27

YOU ought to know better!

The word 'you' has a dual function in our everyday speech. It can generate heat or light. When it's used in a positive way, with the right language, it is relationship enhancing. But it also has a destructive side and, rather like the word 'why' (see #26), which can sound accusatory, it encourages defensiveness when it's used in a negative way with anger: 'You are this!'; 'You are that'; 'You did this.'; 'You did that'.

I feel sure you're familiar with (or have used) words like these:

'*You* always find something nice to say about Fiona's appearance but never mine.'

'*You* never call when you say you're going to and I'm always on tenterhooks.'

'*You* should make more of an effort with the client presentations, even if the decision maker isn't present.'

Notice how these statements also have the 'definitives', to make matters worse – words such as *never, ought, should* and *always*. Instead try:

'Fiona often gets compliments about her dresses, I don't.'

'It's unsettling for me when I don't hear from you on the day that I'm told to expect the call.'

'Even if the decision maker isn't there it's worth putting in the same effort, because they have some influence.'

How many times have you been told, or have you begun a statement like this: 'You make me feel . . .'? There are a number of words we can insert next: useless, worthless, a failure, incensed, inadequate.

So what we're saying is that we've handed control of our emotions to a third party. This inevitably – as with most conflicts – involves *denial* by the other person, in this case on two counts:

1. the action itself
2. the idea that it's their fault that you *feel* a certain way.

The focus then is on 'fault' – and the downward spiral begins.

Be aware of your phrases that begin with the pronoun 'you'. These 'you statements' give out the message that the listener is personally responsible for something. Nobody likes to be unfairly blamed for something. It affects how people react to you. You want people to make amends – not make an enemy.

28

Put the 'I' in feeling

We discussed the negative power of using 'you' (see #27). In situations of tension, anger and frustration it nearly always provokes either a defensive reaction or counter-attack. Also, it stops people listening.

Thomas Gordon formulated, in the 1970s, the principle of 'I' messages relating to how you feel about a particular situation and the distress it may be causing you. Typically, they'll have the words 'I feel . . .', either at the beginning or elsewhere in the statement.

His model was based on the formula of:

- when you X
- I feel Y
- because Z.

'X' is the behaviour, 'Y' is your feeling and 'Z' represents the consequence.

Imagine a conversation that starts with this:

'I feel uneasy when you don't hand the figures in on time because I'm worried that if we artificially miss our monthly targets – because of incomplete figures – they may impose cuts in our department and reduce our headcount.'

The advantage of this technique is that because your statement is based on your feelings, the other person can't possibly disagree with you or start an argument. After all, it's something you personally are *experiencing*. You're taking responsibility for your feelings. You're not blaming the other person about something as you are when hurling 'you' statements that are personal. ('You are sloppy in your report taking.' 'You always leave wet towels around the house.')

Be careful not to slip in *disguised* 'you' accusations along with 'I feel', as it destroys the principle. For example: 'I *feel* that *you* are not concerned about my opinions during meetings.' Better would be: 'I feel ignored during our meetings.' And instead of: 'I feel that you care more about your laptop than talking to me.' try: 'I feel bereft in the evenings, as though I'm on my own.'

Remember, it's a subtle and sincere way of addressing a person about something that is causing you discomfort, and the key to its success is that it is non-judgemental. At the same time, you're indicating the *effect* the other person's actions are having on you.

A member of the team forgets to call an important client as promised, due to child care problems that morning. Avoid being judgemental. Highlight the effects of the error.

Judgemental: 'Well that's the end of all the goodwill we've built up with RBC. You've blown it Julia, because you can't handle your personal life.'

Effects: 'I feel that we've lost all the goodwill with RBC now, Julia. Better call them and apologise profusely. Tell them what your problem was and see if you can try and salvage some business.'

You'll have noticed that using the 'I' statement helps the relationship element of your interaction as well as limiting any damage to a person's self-worth or self-esteem.

Finally, my 'I' message to *you*: 'I' feel concerned that after you've read this book you may forget to use 'I' statements and revert back to 'you'. This may prevent you from having better relationships. So please be aware.

Can I make a
suggestion . . . ?

It's long been thought that the power of suggestion is an important part of our lives, either through our own 'self-talk' or what we hear from others. It has a bearing on how effective we are in reaching our goals or, on the flipside, it can derail any hope of success.

A study in psychological science by Maryanne Garry *et al* highlights the strong influence of 'response expectancies'. This relates to the observation that when something is suggested, or we expect a particular result to occur, we – through our thoughts and reactions – actually make that event occur.

For example, you may say to your teenage child:

'You're probably not a natural driver. Don't be disheartened or ashamed if you *don't* pass this time.'

Contrast that with:

'With your determined streak you'll sail through the driving test next month.'

Or in a work situation you might say:

'Everything's riding on that presentation next week Tim. *Don't* mess up on the figures.'

Contrast that with:

'Tim, I feel confident that you'll give a great presentation to PPR next week. Give them convincing figures so that they feel comfortable with a decision.'

When people suggest we'll 'sail through the driving test' or we'll 'give a great presentation' we're more likely to do whatever it takes to achieve these outcomes. The power of suggestion means our focus is on these positive words.

Conversely, look at those initial statements: '*Don't* be disheartened . . . ashamed' if you '*don't* pass this time.' '*Don't* mess up on the figures.'

The power of suggestion means that we focus on the words that *follow* the 'don't' statement and consequently we're focused on the wrong thing – the negative thing. When you hear statements like these, don't (oops!), or should I say, just challenge the statement with the person (or internally if it's your *thinking* – your self-talk – doing the sabotaging) and change expectations. Here's another example of two contrasting statements:

'Try and enjoy the dinner tonight. *Don't* be rude or disrespectful if they start berating you after you've had your say.'

'Enjoy the reunion dinner tonight Alice and I've got no doubt that, because you're a sensitive person, you'll say the right things, even if comments are made after you've given your little speech.'

So stop and think before issuing your commands. It's far better to focus on the 'positive' side of a situation. When we issue 'don't' commands we're programming the brain to concentrate on the unintended instruction.

(Take a look at the next chapter with the famous experiment involving a white bear. Disclaimer: *no animals were harmed in the process!*)

30

Don't tell me about the 'white bear'

'Try to pose for yourself this task: not to think of a polar bear, and you will see that the cursed thing will come to mind every minute.'
Dostoevsky, 'Winter Notes on Summer Impressions' (1863)

More than a century later it was research at Harvard University by Daniel Wegner that proved the point. He came across this sentence in the book he was reading and it triggered an urge. He wanted to conduct a simple experiment to test the validity of the quote.

Participants in the research were asked to verbalise on anything for five minutes while trying not to think of a white bear (*'Don't think of a white bear'*). Should a white bear pop up in their thoughts, the instruction was to ring a bell.

The group thought of a white bear – despite being instructed not to – on average more than once a minute.

The second exercise involved two groups, and the *original* group was asked to do the same exercise but this time they were told to try to think of a white bear.

The results showed that they thought of a white bear even more often than a second group that had been instructed right from the very beginning to think of white bears.

The research proved that trying *not* to think of something, as the original group did for the first five minutes, causes it to 'rebound' *more* into the mind later on. The results led Wegner to open up and research a new field of study called 'thought suppression'.

His later theory of 'ironic processes' threw up evidence that when trying not to think of something a certain part of the brain avoids the thought, but another part keeps watch every now and then to make sure that the thought does not reappear. Ironically, this only serves to bring the thought *back* into the mind.

'*Sorry* seems to be the hardest word'

We all make mistakes. We end up doing a lot of apologising along the way in life. Cast your mind back to childhood when a 'grown-up' asked you to say 'sorry' for something. It wasn't being in trouble and the awkward situation you were in that caused you distress – it was usually having to apologise to someone.

'I'm sorry'. Two simple words and yet two of the hardest to say.

We easily utter the words in response to trivial matters – bumping into a stranger on the train, tripping over an unmanned supermarket trolley (!), giving a cashier the wrong change. Yet in important matters and to those who mean the most to us, we can find ourselves choking on our words. But our reluctance to apologise – or apologise in the *right* way – can wound all of our relationships with family, friends and work colleagues.

There is no 'blueprint' for a successful apology. Individuals and circumstances are all so different. What we can do is understand the reasons for feeling uncomfortable about uttering words that may help damaged relationships.

Why is it so hard? Often there are four main reasons that are cited:

1. Pride: one of the biggest causes of failure when making an apology – or choosing not to – is pride. To apologise you have to acknowledge that you did something wrong and many find it hard to admit that they made a mistake and made a mess of things.
2. Low empathy (and emotional intelligence): people that fall into this category fail to feel the hurt and distress of another person. Their pride suffers because the other person whom they have offended is antagonistic towards *them*.
3. Embarrassment: the unease with their previous behaviour means they find it difficult to talk about it and so they just pretend it didn't happen.
4. Anger – OK, their actions didn't help but they feel the other person did wrong as well. They feel their anger is justified, so there's inertia.

Yet even when some people deign to apologise, it's done in an insincere way. This is worse than no apology. As I'm sure you've witnessed, at some time, you compound the other person's anger when it's said without sincerity and even worse when it's delivered with an 'escape hatch', as in statements such as: 'I'm sorry you *feel* that I . . .'.

This 'non-apology' (see #32) doesn't admit any liability or blame as the words are saying that they're sorry that the *person* is hurt or angry. In other words, they're not apologising for their misdeeds but simply saying they're sorry that the person is *feeling* certain emotions!

Another favourite is something along the lines of: 'I'm sorry if it caused you any distress'.

The word *any* denotes a lack of thought on the part of the offender as to what kind of effect their actions had on the person. Statements like these antagonise the recipient and tend to make matters worse. They're impersonal and sound like generic proclamations from on high.

Then there's the apology with the focus on the offendee rather than the offended. He or she is sorry that you dislike *them* after their actions that harmed you. Not for the actions they inflicted. So you may get a statement along the lines of: 'I am sorry that you are upset with me' (rather than '*I am sorry I caused you pain*').

If you want an apology to be taken seriously, aim to be *specific*. Show them you:

1. understand what you did wrong, and
2. the effect it had on them, and offer
3. any reassurance for the future (if relevant).

'I'm sorry our lettings office didn't call you about the new instruction (1). I realise it meant you missed out on something suitable, especially as penthouse flats are few and far between (2). Let me make sure in future that we have all your telephone contact details (3).'

'I shouldn't have told Alex you definitely would be interested in going (1). I know you're going to have to give up your piano evening now – I should have remembered (2). It won't happen again, I'm really sorry (3).'

There seems to be a block to many people's desire to apologise because they believe that it is a sign of weakness and admission of guilt. It's been pointed out that, far from displaying 'weakness', having the courage to put yourself in a position that causes you emotional discomfort as you experience shame, and possible retaliation, is a display of strength.

It's the effect your words and actions have on other people that counts. Don't forget that the 'paralanguage' is especially important when you're saying sorry. Your words obviously need to be well-considered but it's the tone and body language that accompany them that decide how effective your statement is. Make sure your eye contact is good and keep your limbs close to your body. Sometimes in life the relationship is more important than the argument.

So be aware of the phrasing of your words of remorse. If you want to give an apology, and you mean it – be authentic. Remember: trust is like a vase. Once it's broken, though you can fix it the vase will never be the same again.

The 'non-apology' apology

If we're not dispensing one, at other times we're complaining about an apology somebody else gave. We seem to inhabit a society that has contradictory views on apologies.

Leaving aside our private lives for the moment, we're often contemplating how people say 'sorry' in the worlds of business and politics – two areas, experience shows us, where the perpetrators fear that an apology shows weakness. For that reason people in positions of power, be it in government or business, tend not to make apologies quickly.

An apology can make the person look weak, and it highlights the fact that they made a mistake or that they're incompetent or not to be trusted. They have to weigh up the consequences of an apology on their image and capacity to stay in a job – and, in some cases, their ability to lead.

So, enter the emergence of the *'non-apology'* apology.

Some people just find it distasteful, through fear or arrogance, to apologise in a direct and sincere way. Why might this be?

A very interesting study conducted by The University of Queensland Business School, into the psychological origins of the 'non-apology' apology, came up with this conclusion:

'. . . Not apologising results in a boost to the person's self-esteem.'

Well, it's probably something that we can all identify with. But at what cost? Pride and self-esteem preserved, but relationships destroyed in personal and professional lives.

Politicians are masters of 'distancing' themselves from a situation while acknowledging some sort of error or misdemeanour has occurred. So, no formal apology – just a linguistic crutch such as *'mistakes were made'*.

The non-apology is sometimes made even *worse* when the person appears to not even acknowledge there is anything wrong, by prefacing the statement with the two-letter, hypothetical word 'if': '. . . *if* mistakes were made'.

We can learn a lot from the way that these 'non-apology' apologies are delivered. The antagonism it causes when people feel their hurt hasn't been *acknowledged*. Are you sometimes guilty of delivering an apology in this way to friends, family, work colleagues or business associates?

Can you recall hearing or making an apology in this manner? It often uses the word 'sorry' combined with our small, two-letter word 'if':

'I'm *sorry if* I offended anyone . . .'

'I *apologise if* anybody was hurt by my actions . . .'

'I'm *sorry if* you feel I haven't handled this well . . .'

This transparent 'non-apology' apology effectively tells you they are sorry for being caught or being criticised – not for what they actually said or did. There is no remorse for actions. Their objective is to placate the other person *and* protect themselves.

Whenever 'if' is included in an 'apology' we can assume the person is not genuinely sorry. Anytime you include this word or any other *modifier* to an attempted apology it makes it a 'non-apology' apology.

If you're going to express that you're sorry for something you said or did, make sure you don't express yourself with this *faux* apology, which often compounds the original problem.

Telephone talk

We're always making telephone calls for business or personal reasons. There's a huge difference between the casual chat we have with friends and family and the type of calls we make and receive in the world of work.

When talking on the telephone, all of the opinions about you are based on the way you sound. Some research has shown that as much as 80 per cent of the assessment is based on the tone of voice of the speaker.

Carefully crafted words cannot disguise your emotions, which are revealed through the tone of your voice. How you feel affects your tone and this can easily be misinterpreted. If you're tired, for example, your voice may display lethargy, which can easily convey the wrong attitude – disinterest and rudeness.

You can convey the wrong impression through your voice when it's obvious that you're multitasking while on the phone. Whether you're having an intermittent conversation with someone in the room or typing an email, the person on the other end of the line may be aware that they don't have your full attention.

A study by London's City University into *prosody* – the rhythm, stress and intonation of speech – reiterated that this was key to how what people say is received. The lead researcher said:

'These features can give us a great deal of information, including how the speaker is feeling at the time and how they feel towards us, the listener. We have all experienced situations where someone's words could have been taken a number of different ways, but their tone has offended us. Hence people remark "it's not what he said, it's the way he said it".'

US researchers at the University of Michigan conducted a study on how speech patterns sway opinions; the findings are applicable to all real-life situations. They studied the recordings of 100 male and female telephone interviewers who made 1,400 calls to convince people to participate in phone surveys.

They looked at the interviewers' speech rates, fluency and pitch and how successful they were in convincing people to participate.

Those who spoke *moderately quickly* – a rate of around 3.5 words per second – were more convincing than those who spoke very quickly or very slowly.

People who spoke too quickly were seen as 'trying to pull wool over our eyes', while those who talked very slowly were perceived as 'not too bright or overly pedantic'.

In addition, the interviewers who paused frequently – around four or five times a minute – were more successful than those who were fluent. The latter were regarded as 'too scripted'.

Sometimes, if you take a call and you have a pressing schedule and know how much time you're able to spare – *let the other person know how long you've got*. It's better than ending a call abruptly by saying words to the effect of 'I've got to go', as that can give the wrong impression.

Just as people find it difficult to end conversations face-to-face, as discussed elsewhere (**see #35**), you probably encounter the same difficulty over the telephone. OK, let's be pragmatic about this: sometimes it's you and sometimes it's the other person! Anyhow, it can be a friend, relative or a business call in which the other person is meandering without getting to the point – or shows no sign of wanting to end the call. Maybe they're waiting for you to provide the signal.

So intervene and conduct it with goodwill, just as you would in a face-to-face situation. People remember beginnings and endings (**remember the primacy and recency effect – see #6?**):

'Good to talk to you Rebecca, you'd better get back to Felicity. I'll dig out those old photos and email them to you.'

'Thanks for spending the time to explain the plans Richard. That's all I need. I've a much better idea now and I'll get some costings by Wednesday.'

Remember – the telephone can convey emotions such as enthusiasm, energy and excitement much better than a text or email.

Networking or 'notworking'?

'These conversationalists say the most shallow and needless of things, impart aimless information, simulate interest they do not feel, and generally impugn their claim to be considered reasonable creatures . . .'

H.G. Wells, 'Of Conversation: An Apology' (1901)

Of course, it's hard to overcome the scenario that may often greet you at many 'networking'-type events: lots of people all talking to each other, looking joyous, pensive, excited or engrossed. And many of them in 'excluding' body-language positions.

They're all coping with the situation well – it's just you.

Dean Martin may have said '*I drink to make other people more interesting*', but we have to use different tactics!

Well, when you ask most people how they feel when they enter into a situation like this you'll tend to find that they feel exactly the same. All they see are people talking to each other with a multitude of facial expressions. Yet, all of these people had to enter into an opening conversation and eventually be talking one to one or in a group.

Very few of them had this kind of 'inner talk' as they entered the room:

> 'Ah, my favourite situation: a room full of absolute strangers. None of them knows me, so all I've got to do is barge through, catch the eye of the drinks waiter, try not to spill the drink through the cliques, pretend to eat a canapé with dignity, try and infiltrate and interrupt a conversation and tell them what I do and how wonderful I am.'

'Is there a way I can help another person?' should actually be the first thought, not 'Could they be of any use to me?' Speaking about them and their business is the best way to progress. You can find out status early on and this will help determine the style and length of conversation. Remember the maxim: understand the difference between someone who loves to talk and someone who has something to say.

I remember at an event when somebody entered our group and, after he introduced himself, the conversation he had with one of the women in the group (Laura) went along these lines:

LAURA: 'Nice to meet you John.'

JOHN: 'You say that you've been working at the radio station for five years now?'

LAURA: 'Yes, I just had a year or so off for maternity leave.'

JOHN: 'We've been helping to produce adverts for local stations since 1972. I've been there for just over a year now. Was it a boy or a girl?'

LAURA: 'Sorry, what do you mean?'

JOHN: 'I meant your pregnancy – did you have a boy or a girl?'

LAURA: 'Oh, a girl. Sarah, she's just over two now.'

JOHN: 'I'll just give you my card. Would it be possible to meet you and discuss our services for radio adverts?'

LAURA: 'Err . . . I'm not involved with any of that. I'm a PA in the human resources department.'

I know that from my conversations with other people, these introductions seem to be something that causes great discomfort. Generally speaking, it's best to start the conversation by giving your name – s-l-o-w-l-y.

Of course, you can start conversations without this, but you must have been in the situation where you've established some rapport and, halfway through the conversation, you're asking: 'Erm. What's your name?' Or worse, having to ask when you're leaving!

If you come across somebody you've met in the past you can help them avoid the embarrassment of not knowing (or remembering) your name with a remark accompanying your outstretched hand: 'Hi Jeremy . . . Simon' (pause). 'Good to see you.'

The other person can respond as if he knew your name: 'Simon. How's things?' You're not sure whether he remembered your name, but it doesn't matter. You're in a conversation. You may want to get your own back. You can't quite remember who he works for and what his position is, without a prompt. Time for him to make life easier for you (unwittingly!):

SIMON: 'What's been occupying your time at work lately, Jeremy?'

JEREMY: 'Oh. I'm handling plastic extrusions now. There were a few changes after our takeover last month by XYZ.'

(Of course . . .) You've had a memory prompt. Now you remember, he's a civil engineer. 'Let's see, Laser Weld was taken over last month, I remember now.'

Now, when somebody joins the group – after you've introduced yourself you can confidently introduce them to Jeremy Brand from Laser Weld: 'Ah. Laser Weld. We were talking about your company in our project meeting the other day. Have you got a few moments?' Now he's in conversation with somebody else.

Quite often, background noise from humans and music or environmental noise makes it difficult to hear perfectly all the time. You may miss or at least mishear part of the conversation. If you don't ask a person to *repeat* what they've just said the rule is to keep a neutral expression on your face. No forced smiles and head nods if you were unable to hear what the person said. Suppose the words you missed were: '*The bites I got on holiday in Greece turned septic. Just spent two days in hospital.*' Smiling and nodding your head won't endear you!

When it's time to leave a person or a group, try and be the one who's talking as you take your leave. It's a smoother transition.

Exit 'lines'

'You have delighted us long enough.'

Jane Austen, *Pride and Prejudice*

You need to finish talking with someone in a positive way. Sometimes that natural point in which you (or both of you) feel the need to close a conversation has already passed and so there's a slight awkwardness or anxiety that's rippling under the surface.

Bearing in mind the 'recency' effect (see #25), people tend to remember the last elements of interaction and how they felt at the time. Take heed of the statement:

People may not remember what you said but they remember how you made them feel.

Therefore it's important, if possible, to end a discussion in a pleasant manner. Wait for the natural junctions and any pauses that occur in any conversation.

You or the other person may need to move on. In their case you may sense a slight awkwardness in their trying to indicate that – for fear of causing offence. So make it easy for them, for example by saying:

'I don't want to monopolise your time . . .'

'I need to be thinking about making a move . . .'

'It's been really good to talk with you.'

If it's you that needs to bring the discussion to a close then you can indicate that you've been paying attention – and therefore found the conversation useful – by giving a recap of the main points of your talk: 'That's interesting to hear that you feel there'll be . . .'.

The way you end your interaction will, in some part, be responsible for the person's memory of your conversation. As such, it's important.

There's a delicate line to tread because at all times we don't want to give an impression that is totally unfounded and causes offence. The point is, everything ends – even conversations! That doesn't mean one or the other of you is boring. There's no element of rejection.

The best time is after you have finished talking. It's a natural time to make your leave. If you leave immediately after the other person has spoken or during the middle of it, they may think it's related to their talk.

At the same time, if there is scope for meeting again, mention this. Try this, the next time that you're in a situation where you want to exit a conversation you're having with somebody.

The other person will recognise this signal of intent that you are about to leave – and you've left them with the impression that you're sincere and a good listener! *You have delighted them long enough!*

Mirroring?
('*yeah, yeah, yeah*')

We 'mirror' other people when we achieve a degree of rapport with them. There naturally occurs a degree of *matching* of body language.

There's also evidence that *speech patterns* feature in our innate desire for bonding. When we feel that someone shares similar values with us, we align ourselves with their speech patterns. Researchers found that human brains imitate the speech patterns of other people, without meaning to, from an inbuilt urge of the brain to 'empathise and affiliate'. The scientists at University of California, Riverside say that '*humans are incessant imitators . . . we imitate each other's speech patterns, including inflections, talking speed and speaking time*'.

If you speak quickly and you're in conversation with someone whose speech pattern is much slower, *then slow down* to match the other person's speech pattern for the first few minutes. This makes the other person feel more at ease. Then you can increase it to an optimum rate.

You can also make people feel more at ease by using the same type of *language* they use. Notice whether people are using long, complex sentences or short, simple ones and modify your speech to theirs. They'll feel more comfortable conversing with you.

What about colloquialisms? Maybe you're talking in a group or meeting and you suddenly become aware that you're the only person using a much-used word, or words, in their pure form.

For example, I remember being in a meeting with a colleague talking with a number of advertising agency creatives and the account management team – he was doing the main presentation. They were quite casual in their speech (and dress) – all using the colloquial 'yeah' multiple times in a minute. My colleague was using the more formal 'yes' repeatedly. It stood out so much and just seemed incongruent. As we finished that meeting I can recall saying: 'Yeah, we'll get back to you tomorrow'.

Paul McCartney recounts a tale regarding The Beatles' 1963 hit 'She Loves You'. He describes how the band were at his family home in Liverpool and had just finished writing the song and then sought the advice of his father, also an accomplished musician – Jim McCartney:

'We went into the living room. I said "Dad, listen to this. What do you think?" So we played it to my dad and he said: "That's very nice son, but there's enough of these Americanisms around. Couldn't you sing "She loves you, yes yes yes!" At which point we collapsed in a heap and said "No dad, you don't quite get it!".'

The astute 'foursome' obviously identified well with their teenage audience as this became The Beatles' biggest-selling single in the UK under the astute guidance of producer George Martin. 'Yeah, yeah, yeah' became the group's catchphrase – they became known throughout Europe as the 'Yeah-Yeahs'. Headlines, posters, T-shirts and memorabilia around the world had these words printed on them. The song with this refrain, which was perceived to be very informal at the time (though much more colloquial now, of course), was used as a musical hook and is heard 15 times in the short 2 minutes 21 seconds of the song.

When we feel that someone shares similar values with us, we align ourselves with their speech patterns. Make sure it happens *naturally*. Be aware of your authentic self.

37

Are you a 'radiator' or a 'drain'?

Oprah Winfrey was asked about the one thing that she wished she'd learned earlier on in life. Her response was: '*I wish I'd learned how to distinguish radiators from drains*'.

Think of the people in your life that you like and look forward to seeing. It can be family, friends, work colleagues, neighbours, store employees, anyone. Chances are it's their warmth, vitality and a positive outlook. You feel able to talk about anything and are comfortable in their company.

These are the 'radiators' in your life. These people make you feel good about this world that we live in. Their speech is generally positive and uplifting. They may mention late trains and creaky knees but they won't slide into a morbid discussion on the breakdown of society and destruction of the planet. They don't stonewall you with a barrage of negativity, and tend to concentrate on *solutions* to their problems rather than infecting you with the contagion. Conversations with these people leave you feeling uplifted and energised as they radiate warmth in their conversations.

Conversely, what about those people in your life who sap your energy, leaving you feeling drained? These are the 'drains'. It's their negative words and demeanour that give you the feeling that you're getting *less* out of the interaction than they are. (Have you given up being friends with someone after a while because of the realisation that they have this kind of effect on you?)

Their downbeat conversation and addiction to relaying bad news creates a negative atmosphere, which – if you stick around long enough – gradually infects you, leaving you feeling pessimistic about life (and you were OK before!).

Such is the effect of this '*neural mirroring*', as neuroscientists have termed it – when we pick up the mood of those around us. In the case of drains, that's not an ideal state for us. But, on the flip side, it also means that our mirror neurons leave us feeling *good* after being in the presence of radiators.

What about you? Are you aware of your attitude and how it affects others around you? Be aware of how you converse with people. We all lapse momentarily from time to time into the drain mode, but overall make sure you're coming across as radiating warmth and positivity. Keep a check on your plumbing! Also, make sure you exhibit open and warm body language to accompany your energising words.

38

Say 'yes' to 'no'

The word 'no' is usually the first word that young toddlers learn; and this holds true in most languages.

In any social or work context it's difficult to say 'no' or to say it assertively. In a social context it may be appropriate without giving reasons, but in the working world refusing and giving acceptable reasons why is important – because it has a bearing on relationships.

How many relationships have been ruined through being unable to say 'no'?

Not to mention the relationships at home as you take on too much work, thus upsetting your work–life balance.

You need to draw a distinction in your replies as to what you are saying, and make sure that the other person is aware of the difference. There are two factors at play:

- you say you 'can't' (which means you're not able) or
- you 'won't' (which means you don't want to).

How many times have you come across people bemoaning the fact that they've said 'yes' to a request and then rue the decision as they deal with the pressure and resentment? All self-induced because they find it difficult to say 'no'.

Sometimes it's because you've been put on the spot and you're in the middle of something, maybe, and you can't, in the heat of the moment, summon up the right words to refuse. So the quick option is to agree. Not a satisfying reason for agreeing to do something.

It's perfectly acceptable, in many instances, to ask for some time before coming back to them if you need to check something before making a decision:

> 'I need to see whether I've committed myself that evening to a school function for James. Let's talk tomorrow.'

> 'Of course I'd like to help you out since you're one short in the department. I'll need to see how urgently they want those advertising figures from me.'

Invariably, the conflict – when someone asks you to help on a task or when they 'choose' you for a project – arises because you're trying to preserve a 'relationship', whether that be personal or business. If you feel that you want to help but at a more convenient time, then bring that to the person's attention as it gives authenticity to your refusal and helps in the relationship element:

> 'If you're planning another trip to the theatre later this month, Sophie, I'd be happy to babysit for you then.'

> 'See if you can get HR to switch your meeting to the afternoon on Friday and then I'll happily give you a hand in the morning.'

Increasingly, I've come across people who when asked 'What do you most dislike about yourself?' answer, 'I say "yes" too often' or 'Sometimes I accept things and think: "*what did I do that for?*"'.

Typical thoughts going through your head as to why you can't refuse may be:

- they'll be hurt if I say no
- they'll be angry with me if I refuse
- they won't like me
- it will look as though I can't cope.

There are also the typical stages you may go through after not being able to refuse a request:

1. It's a voluntary task or project that you're asked to help with and you don't want to *disappoint* a colleague or friend.
2. You agree to take it on, but because of other commitments you're not able to give it your *best* efforts.
3. You end up *resenting* doing it.
4. You apportion blame to the *person* who made the *request.*

And this is all because you couldn't summon up a gracious way to phrase a 'no' to a friend or colleague.

You can highlight the problems that will occur for you if you agree to their request:

> 'I'm so sorry but if I do X it will mean . . .'

> 'I won't be able to do that because Tuesdays are my fixed days for . . .'

> 'I feel honoured that you asked me, but the schedule won't allow it . . .'

Sometimes it's a moral or 'principle' reason that makes you decline:

> 'No, I don't feel comfortable . . .'

'No, I'd rather not participate.'

'No, thanks for asking but I've decided not to.'

Sometimes you simply may not want to give a *reason*:

'I'm sorry that I can't explain my decision, but the answer is no.'

'I'd be happy to help you but it's a bad time for me.'

'I've decided not to invest after careful consideration . . . but I wish you the best of luck.' (You'll often hear something like this on BBC TV's *Dragon's Den* from one of the investors on the panel.)

Some people perpetuate the situation by using the words 'maybe' or 'might'. Now that's not so bad when there's a genuine possibility, but the problem is that it delays the unease at the time and later you may still end up saying 'no'. As far as the other person is concerned, they're making plans around your wavering decision, but you're going to say 'no' . . . in the end. From a relationship point of view it's better to respond with something like:

'No. Thanks for the thought, but it's not my thing.'

'No. I'd come if I was able, but there's just too much going on with the children at the moment.'

Some people are uncomfortable with the word 'no'. So say it in another way:

'I'm sorry, I'd like to help you out, but it's impossible at the moment.'

'Thanks for asking me but I won't be able to contribute.'

In instances where the relationship element is not paramount, and you simply don't want to engage with a person or a 'cause' that you don't agree with, it's often better to be firm and neutral in your response:

'I've considered it carefully. I don't feel I want to participate. Thanks for . . .'

'No. It's thoughtful of you to think of me. I have my reasons.'

Often, depending on the relationship, you don't have to give an *explanation* for your decision. Explanations tend to open up a dialogue about your reasons for a 'no' and you may sometimes end up tying yourself in knots and having to justify your reasons.

39

Balance honesty with courtesy

'Words – so innocent and powerless as they are, as standing in a dictionary, how potent for good and evil they become, in the hands of one who knows how to combine them!'

Nathaniel Hawthorne

For some people, the honesty element without the courtesy is their trademark style that causes poor communication and fractures relationships. Their comments may be too 'direct' or 'blunt'.

When we say something badly, quite often it's because of our lack of awareness and mindfulness in the moment. In an effort to say things based on how *you feel* at that moment, the statements can be hurtful and insensitive with no regard for the other person's feelings.

Equally, just being 'honest' can be hurtful and insensitive, leading to friction and the message becoming ineffective.

On the flip side, if our talk is based purely on courtesy and avoiding necessary but unpleasant statements then our conversation becomes inauthentic. It's not getting to the point for the sake of avoiding feelings of hurt, anger or discomfort. Messages that are unpleasant are diluted or avoided altogether. Too much 'sugar-coating' hides the 'real' reason, which then causes ineffective and unclear communication:

'Did anybody think to tell me that an answer was needed by Monday morning at the latest?'

You're being honest with your annoyance but, rather than an answer to the question, you're seeking to make an *accusatory* statement. This will inevitably invite defensiveness or an argument – especially if there is a valid reason.

Try and use *statements* rather than questions. It takes the sting out of the demand. So, in the example above, we remove *accusation* and concentrate on how we're *thinking* and *feeling*:

'It would have helped me if I'd been advised that they needed an answer by Monday morning.'

The statement has been made in a more courteous way and still seeks information, which may or may not provide a valid reason. But the tone of the conversation will take a *different* turn.

There are certain phrases that are 'favourites' for feigning courtesy and usually have the opposite effect on the listener. Here are a few to avoid in your conversations:

- 'With all due respect' – in most cases this usually precedes passive/ aggressive communication and is not offering respect at all! You'll see and hear it in political interviews a lot. (The subtext is usually along the lines of 'how ignorant can you be; I'll explain this again until I batter you into submission . . .'.)
- 'What you have to understand is' – we don't have to understand anything. Instead you can implore: 'What I hope you understand is . . . .'. That's courteous.
- 'You need to' – rather like the previous statement, you're telling someone what to do.
- 'Don't take this the wrong way' or 'don't take this personally' – whenever you hear these phrases, it hardly ever stops you taking it 'the wrong way' or 'personally'! You know that it's going to be a precursor to some kind of criticism or 'feedback' that will be personal to you; and upsetting! *Few people can remember the words that come directly after this phrase*; the brain puts you in fight/flight mode. It's certainly a phrase to be wary of if you're giving feedback as a manager. Whether it's in your working or personal life, try and eliminate these five phrases.

Effective talk combines a *balance* of honesty with courtesy. They work in tandem to make conversations productive and to avoid bad feeling. Therefore you're able to be truthful and be gracious in how you make your case. Always remember, fragile human beings that we are, that feelings come first, logic second.

40

'To be honest' it's 'no problem'

Y ou know when you come across phrases uttered by someone that subconsciously make you feel uneasy? What about '*to be honest*' or '*honestly*' or '*if I'm honest*'? What effect do these 'honesty' phrases have on you?

'To be honest', or similar variations, is something we hear when talking to friends and family, people at work and when listening to public figures on the media. It's endemic.

Think about when you're engaged in conversation with someone, or you're listening to a speech and then you hear the words: '*Well, to be honest with you* . . .'. What's the implication? What does that mean?

Are they saying: 'Listen carefully. Change of tactics. I'm now going to start telling the truth!'

'To be honest, I'd change the whole roof structure if I was you, not just the slates.'

'To be honest I think you should go for this one.'

'Honestly, we're the best firm in the area when it comes to quality of work.'

In most instances we're not even questioning the 'honesty rating' of people that may begin their statements this way. What it does for the listener, though, is to instil a sense of doubt about the person's relationship with the truth. It implies that anything said before was untrue.

It's a 'loaded' word in psycholinguistic terms. And it's totally unnecessary!

When you hear someone using it repeatedly (watch for it next time) it compounds the doubt in your mind. What's the effect of a conversation like this:

BUILDER: '*To be honest*, I think you should go for this one.'

CUSTOMER: 'Isn't that the more expensive one?'

BUILDER: 'It is, *in all honesty*. But you get what you pay for.'

CUSTOMER: 'Didn't your colleague yesterday say that the most expensive was not necessarily the best for our purposes?'

BUILDER: 'He might have. You could go for the cheaper one I suppose. *To be perfectly honest*, there's not much in it between the two.'

(That's three '*honests*' – and counting. By the way, didn't the builder propose the more expensive one earlier on!?)

In this example there was no previous referral to a person's integrity, such that he should have begun his conversation announcing his honesty.

Scientific studies have shown that when a person showcases their honesty at the beginning of a statement, in many instances it's because they are aware they are engaging in deception.

In other cases, these words are uttered as a verbal *crutch*. Since how we determine meaning is based on perception and the subconscious, even if you use these words *innocently*, it may be wise to eliminate them from your statements. They can alert the listener to *look* for clues of deception.

There's another growing affliction that's at large. Let's describe it as the knee-jerk response of '*no problem*'. What is the *problem* with 'no problem'? It's fine in our *informal* conversations. It's when it's being used in professional instances, when an action or service offered shouldn't even be an *inconvenience*, that it becomes an issue.

In these instances, it sounds abrupt – and it's inaccurate.

For example, you're in a restaurant and your first course of soup arrives for you and your partner but the cutlery that was so flamboyantly arranged in front of you, after your order was taken, doesn't include a spoon. You catch the waiter's eye, eventually.

'Thank you' is your polite response to the waiter as he brings two spoons to your table. 'No problem' is his reply. (Requiring a spoon to eat soup shouldn't have constituted a 'problem' anyway!)

Or what about the two sales assistants chatting by the cash desk while you're standing there waiting to purchase an item (silently fuming and resisting the urge to mutter under your breath). Finally, when hope looks slim, you say: 'Excuse me. Could I just pay for this blouse?'

One of the two girls interrupts her conversation, gives you a big smile and, as she aims the item of clothing towards the barcode reader, says 'No problem'.

Well, maybe some retail stores should be enlightening their retail staff that a customer wanting to buy an item is certainly not a 'problem' (quite the reverse if the establishment wants to stay in business!).

What about in the office? Maybe you're a manager who's had to reprimand (in a fair way) one of your team for consistently doing something incorrectly and causing repercussions for the department. 'So,

John, can you please double check each invoice before you send them out in future please?' 'No problem.' (Was that a reassuring and appropriate response from somebody who obviously *does* find it a problem?)

You're in a delicate meeting with one of your suppliers and they're not too pleased with recent deliveries because of problems that have repeatedly occurred:

> CLIENT: 'We've had a good relationship with you for many years but over the last year, as you know, your deliveries – the last four in fact – have included a number of broken items, which means we're letting down our customers with the dates we're quoting. Could you make sure we don't suffer with this again?'
>
> YOU: 'Yes. No problem.'

(If there was no problem, the conversation wouldn't even be taking place!)

So be aware of this phrase in more *formal* situations and only use it in instances when you are going above and beyond what you might be expected to do.

Be aware that when a 'no problem' response is given, the focus is on a word with a *negative* connotation (the word 'problem' is not an attractive one, neurologically). It can sound as though the task that was completed for the person was an imposition of some sort.

Think back to your own experiences. What about when you hear 'it's my pleasure', which has a *positive* ring to it? Equally, 'you're welcome' is sufficiently courteous.

41

'Um' . . . 'err' . . . 'uh' . . . target the killer 'fillers'

L inguists use the term 'fillers' for those *sounds, words* and *phrases* that act like a pause mid-sentence, giving the speaker time to gather their thoughts while signalling to the listener that they still want the listener's attention.

We can't keep up with our own thoughts much of the time and so we need to pause and think. But if there's too much use of fillers it can give the impression of nervousness or that the person needs time to think about something. Or that they're unprepared.

Let's look at the typical filler 'sounds'. The ones that come in for a lot of criticism are sounds such as 'uh', 'err' and 'um'. The pattern seems to be that with habit it becomes normal for people to use these fillers and they don't know they're using them, until it's pointed out to them.

The use of these in *moderation* does no harm. It's the repeated and excessive use that is distracting for an audience.

Researchers at Stanford University say they find that these disfluencies – when used in moderation – may also serve a role for listeners: 'If we anticipate a delay in our speech, we choose the appropriate sound to signal this to the listener. By signalling a delay is coming, a speaker avoids a silent gap in conversation that might otherwise prove confusing to a listener.'

Their research shows that the 'um' and 'err' sounds usually set up a *long* delay in speech, while the 'uh' usually signals only a *brief* pause.

Why do we use some of these filler sounds?

• Often we don't want someone else to start speaking, we're not finished.
• In some instances we feel pressure to start speaking quickly.

If you're unprepared (for a speech or presentation, for example) that's when the filler sounds become more prolific. You tend to be more nervous when you have skipped on the preparation and nerves make most people's *pace* change – *you speak quicker and your brain can't keep up*.

Speaking of pace, just reducing this a little in everyday speech should reduce the ums, errs and uhs, because the brain will find it easier to keep up with you.

As well as sounds, we use filler words and phrases that add nothing to our sentences, such as:

I mean

sort of

you know

kind of

well

like

basically

literally

you know what I mean

are you following what I'm saying

you get my point

and numerous others.

These words and phrases are sometimes referred to as 'discourse markers' – removing them still leaves the sentence structure intact. We tend to use them more when speaking informally, when damage is limited. They're common in informal speech.

In more formal settings and in business and the workplace these words can make you seem unsure of your ideas. Try and avoid them, as the perception created may be one of lack of preparation or knowledge on your part – whether fairly or unfairly. Try and self-monitor your use of 'fillers' and remember that knowledge and preparation – and altering the pace (paralanguage) of your speech – can help reduce those unwanted sounds and words.

42

Hold the jargon

*'Speketh so pleyn at this time, we yow preye, that we may under-
stonde what ye seye.'*

Geoffrey Chaucer, *'Prologue to the Clerk's Tale'*,
Canterbury Tales (late 14th century)

Here's the 'Modern English' version of this statement:

*'Speak plainly at this time, we beg you, so that we may
understand the words you say.'*

Jargon (and its close cousin 'business speak') in and of itself is neither
a good or bad thing. In its purest form, jargon, the specialised language
used by people in the same type of work or profession, should be something used as a form of shorthand. It's rife in the workplace and many
managers use it without considering the impact it has on their staff. But
jargon often results in excluding people from discussions. It's no longer
just confined to consultants, the finance world and business-school
types; and wherever it is, it undermines trust.

There seems to be the feeling that using management jargon makes
you a good manager. One of the keys to engaging, motivating and
enthusing people is to communicate in a way that everyone can easily
understand.

The problem with jargon is the 'sender' not the 'receiver'. How aware
are you that you're using these words when you're talking to people?

If jargon is being used not to aid communication but to impress
your 'audience' and to sound knowledgeable and important, then the
communication suffers. The corporate world is now rife with its close
cousin, 'business speak', which irritates or mesmerises audiences. It's
often used as a substitute for thinking. Let's create some three-letter
acronyms. Or better still, let's toss out some 'low-hanging fruit' and
let the audience feast!

In an article in the *Financial Times* (13 December 2007) the writer
noted that jargon: 'can turn a bunch of windbags in a meeting room into
a "quick wins taskforce".' He goes on to say: 'I once asked a handyman
toiling in an office doorway whether he was installing a wheelchair
ramp. "No" he said solemnly, "it's a diversity access feature".'

Professor Roy Baumeister (Florida State University) reminds us that
there is specialist language used in all walks of life. He defends the use
of jargon: *'Jargon has a positive function . . . everyday terms are used in
fuzzy and sloppy ways and carry lots of connotational baggage. Jargon
is used because it is precise. New terms can be defined carefully . . .'*

That's all well and good. But of course we rely on industry professionals to translate technical 'shorthand' language used in an industry or organisation into a form that is clear to us. For example, most of us, through constantly hearing the term 'quantitative easing', have developed an idea as to its broad meaning:

DAN FOREMAN: 'Guys, I feel very terrible about what I'm about to
                say. But I'm afraid you're both being let go.'

LOU: 'Let go? What does that mean?'

DAN FOREMAN: 'It means you're being fired.'

(In Good Company, 2004)

Most of us recognise 'business speak', with its ubiquitous terms. Here are just a few:

going forward

drill down

think outside the box

no brainer

reach out

interface with clients

low-hanging fruit

drill down

touch base

in the long run.

'Transitioning' is another word now often used in business. Heard it lately? Angela Ahrendts, who moved from being CEO of Burberry to join Apple, used the word to describe her move, defining it as: '*moving from past and present to future, professionally and personally*'. The word is often used to give 'change' extra gravitas.

The Plain English Campaign says that many employees use long words to impress and bluff, quite often not even knowing what these words mean. They conduct conversations in and out of meetings and use this management speak to sound impressive. For some, jargon/ business speak is used to show superiority. But not being able to use words other than those in the 'inside language' that's used in their own industry or organisation is something that needs to be addressed. It's not a sign of superior intelligence.

Perhaps these people should remember Albert Einstein's observation:

'If you can't explain an idea to a nine year old, then you don't really understand it.'

The ILM (Institute of Leadership and Management) conducted a survey that revealed that 'management speak' is used in nearly two thirds of offices (64 per cent). Their survey also highlighted the top three overused phrases of jargon:

1. 'thinking outside the box' (57 per cent)
2. 'going forward' (55 per cent)
3. 'let's touch base' (39 per cent).

So 'reaching out' and 'touching base' could easily go back to being 'contact' or 'get in touch', without any loss of *intellectual* status. Maybe at the next management meeting you could even cut out 'delivery' – unless of course you're organising pizza for the lunch!

It's OK if you're a professional dealing with your own colleagues in the same industry or profession and you want to converse with them in this way. It may act for what it was originally intended – as a kind of *verbal shorthand*. It's when it transitions (ugh!) into hiding or distorting information that the problems arise; from easily understood 'in' words and phrases for a particular audience to obfuscation.

We know that politicians may use it to dissemble and avoid searching questions. Remember in 2008 when the financial crisis was rebranded as the 'credit crunch'? What was that all about?!

In business, the use of jargon has come under fire not because of the words themselves but the fact that speakers may fail to consider whether it is appropriate for their audience of one or many.

It's important for you if you're using jargon/business speak to observe the 'listening', non-verbal behaviour of your audience to see whether they are mentally 'switching-off' due to confusion. Few people in a group setting will typically challenge the speaker to clarify words or phrases for fear of embarrassment.

So maybe (if you're guilty through habit), you should think again before reaching for those overused and irritating expressions. Put your career aspirations for oil exploration, fruit picking and delivering pizza on hold!

Perhaps that could be your 'mission statement'?

The magical 'rule of three'

What is it about three that makes it so powerful in conveying information?

Three is the smallest number that there is to form a *pattern*. Our brain is receptive to 'data' that can be processed through recognising a pattern. Because three is a small number it enables a message framed in this way to be memorable.

We're used to being told from childhood that stories have a beginning, middle and an end; the tales are more engaging, and more effectively presented. Similarly, audiences are more likely to consume and absorb any type of information that comes in threes, especially with rhetoric:

> *'... This country does best when everyone gets their fair shot.*
> *Everyone does their fair share.*
> *And everyone plays by the same set of rules.'*

When it comes to speeches, some of the most powerful men in history were using this pattern long ago: 'Friends. Romans. Countrymen', for example, Barack Obama's 'Yes we can' speech included more than twelve of these 'rule-of-three' statements.

Benjamin Franklin famously informed us:

> *'Tell me and I forget.*
> *Teach me and I remember.*
> *Involve me and I learn.'*

Memory research shows we can only retain three to four chunks of information in short-term memory. The use of the rule of three therefore promotes recall. Ever noticed that plays are typically divided into three acts? Advertisers also like to promote their wares in this manner: 'lighter, faster, thinner'; slogans are formulated with the same simple rule – 'Just do it.'

In a 'Charm of three' study carried out in 2013 by researchers at Georgetown University (Washington DC) and the University of California (Los Angeles) they found that making three positive claims was optimal when trying to persuade someone. After three, people became more sceptical. So, when listing potential benefits of a product or proof that an idea will work, *'three claims may be the charm'*, they concluded.

Their research also showed that if you're trying to persuade 'busy' bosses or 'busy senior clients', present three reasons. Why should we do this?

Well, they concluded, 'there are three reasons it's effective . . .' (what, three again?!):

1. you are forced to *choose* the three most important reasons
2. your argument gets their *attention* and is *memorable*
3. you sound more *structured, confident* and *decisive* when you speak.

Here's an example:

'There are three reasons we should take up the offer from this new supplier:

1. they're giving us attractive credit terms
2. they've got a 99.2 per cent credibility rating for on-time delivery
3. Helen Willetts, the new MD, once worked for our company and knows our business well.'

It's memorable when you say in your presentation: *'there are three reasons we should do X . . .'* (Note: if you have a number of topics, you can group them into three categories.)

While we're on the subject of 'threes', I'd like to share with you a style adopted by a former work colleague of mine, which he used to call the '3 plus 1'. He used to use this in client and internal presentations – and also at home with his children, he told me.

The gist of this was three successive *positive* statements, followed at the end with a *negative*-type statement (which warned of *loss* by not heeding the first three).

Here's two illustrations of this:

Statement 1: 'Tom. Your department's produced the best conversion figures for the whole of Northern Europe – it's a 28 per cent increase on last year.'

Statement 2: 'We're consequently no longer on the possible list of closures under the restructuring plan, thanks to your motivational skills.'

Statement 3: 'You can hold your head up high for well-deserved recognition at the regional meeting in San Francisco in a couple of months' time.'

'Keep vigilant on the figures for the upcoming year as it would be a shame if we end up back on the list.' (potential loss)

Statement 1: 'Sarah, your room's looking really tidy these days; you're putting in a lot of effort after mum spoke to you about it.'

Statement 2: 'It's been a lot easier for you to find things now and you haven't missed the train and been late for school at all in the last couple of weeks.'

Statement 3: 'Since Mum hasn't had to drive you to school she's been able to use some of the time on those dresses you wanted her to make – from the magazine.'

'Let's keep the good work up with your room because it would be unfortunate if mum had to abandon this now, as she's quite enjoying reviving her dressmaking skills for you.' (potential loss)

Somewhere in the recesses of our mind, our subconscious makes us amenable to written and verbal messages in threes. Maybe that's because they're:

1. easy to read
2. easy to say
3. easy to remember.

(Do you see what I mean?!)

When we use the rule of three in rhetoric or to present a structure to our arguments it is very *persuasive*.

44

'I'm an extrovert . . . get me in there!'

Many neuroscientific studies have been done on the brains of intro-verts and extroverts and they show that they really are different. A 1999 study, reported in the *American Journal of Psychiatry,* exam-ined the results after a cerebral blood flow of introverted and extro-verted people was conducted. They used PET scans on the subjects, as they thought freely, and discovered the following:

- Introverts had more blood flow in the frontal lobes and anterior thalamus. These are brain regions involved with recalling events, making plans and solving problems.
- Extroverts had more blood flow in the temporal lobes and posterior thalamus. These are areas involved with interpreting sensory data.

The data confirmed, from a neurobiological view, what had always been known:

- the extrovert's attention is focused *outwards*.

The results showed that, in terms of language, extroverts speak differently:

- extroverts talk more *abstractly*.

The test was related to how the two groups described things. The researchers had the participants describe what was happening in the photographs and the introverts were more *precise* in their descriptions.

So, if you have an extroverted personality you can probably be planted in any social situation and at least get the small talk started without feeling too much pain.

Research studies over the last half-century show that, in general, those people with more of an extrovert disposition tend to enjoy group projects and talking through thoughts. They tend to think out loud by talking and interacting with others. Rather unfairly, extroverts are often branded as over-talkative or, in some cases, as attention-seeking. In actual fact it's the case that the extrovert gains energy when they're engaging in any kind of social interaction; they need the social inter-change to get the energy.

Extroverts are more likely to assert themselves in groups and so may often be in leadership or managerial positions where they are working with many people.

A major criticism of the overconfident extrovert is that they need to learn how to talk to the shy or more withdrawn type of person. If an extrovert's natural rate of speaking is quite direct and on the fast side and they're interacting with somebody more on the introversion scale – who may have a much slower rate of talking and likes to deal in detail – it pays to *slow* the rate down to a pace similar to that of the other person.

Match the speech patterns initially and respect the different style. Understand that, as far as content goes, the introverted person likes to digest detail *slowly* at first. This can be carried on until they've built up an element of rapport. After that the extrovert could revert to their more natural style. It's the beginning that is important.

Similarly, with the other 'paralanguage' element of loudness, if you're dealing with someone who speaks quietly then match the style at first in order to get on the same wavelength.

Remember that the more introverted type of person is not prone to display much in the way of body language signals and facial expressions and can appear aloof and reserved. Spend time paraphrasing back to them what you've heard in order to confirm that you've understood their point correctly.

If you're more of the extrovert type you probably have no trouble in conversing with those of a similar disposition to yourself. When dealing with others you have to adapt your speaking and listening style more to theirs during your interactions.

45

'I'm an introvert . . . get me out of here!'

'If animals could speak, the dog would be a blundering outspoken fellow; but the cat would have the rare grace of never saying a word too much.'

Mark Twain

Introversion is a much misunderstood personality trait. There is no right or wrong. Not everyone can easily be described as either an introvert or an extrovert. Generally, 'introverted' describes someone who is more focused on internal thoughts and feelings rather than seeking *external* stimulation (the hallmark of their extrovert counterparts).

It's not the misunderstood 'Greta Garbo' syndrome: they don't always want to be alone! They're just more quiet and reserved and don't want or need to be the centre of attention.

When contrasting the two types, the keyword is 'energy'. Introverts tend to *expend* energy with people, whereas the extrovert type *gains* energy when exposed to people. The introvert often has to 'recharge' by spending some time alone after a group session or a party. As someone once said: 'they have more fun leaving the party'.

However, they can also be excellent public speakers. Giving a talk to 200 people would be less stressful than interacting with members of the audience afterwards. Introverts like to think and communicate – from the inside outwards.

This extract gives an insight into the character of an introvert:

'When talking about economics, MC Williams is fluent – the figures are in easy grasp and the arguments well-oiled. On personal matters his voice is quiet and his words elide.'

Networking is not something that comes easily for this type of person. They prefer to have discussions one to one, or in very small groups.

They tend to be good on detail and, equally, they prefer to *think* about things before talking. In this digital world they may prefer writing an email, for example, rather than making a telephone conversation that requires instant response and no *control* over time and duration and content of talk.

In the working world there may not be too much verbal feedback from this type. It's not a question of poor listening. On the contrary, they tend to be good listeners. Being very good on detail, they tend to need time to process information and then perhaps respond in writing in a methodical way.

Dealing with people of a *similar* disposition – in conversation – is usually much easier for the introverted type. When dealing with others, recognise that you may have to interject during dialogue with the more extroverted type in order to satisfy your need to extract detail. Recognise that your pace of talk is different and that extroverts may speak faster as they *gain* energy during an interchange. They're not necessarily glossing over details; it's their natural style.

Their sentences are probably longer than yours. Just as they may need to adapt to your style eventually, as they get to know you, it pays for you to understand the differences in order for you to build rapport.

Feedback . . . 'How am I doing?'

'I gotta go learn a bunch of people's names before I fire them.'
Roger Stirling, *Mad Men*

Feedback. It's a word we hear all the time now. What was once a 'buzzword' is now an integral part of our lives. Social media has undoubtedly contributed to it becoming a norm in everyday life.

We're all giving and receiving feedback much of the time in various settings. It may not be formal, but just in our everyday interactions with family, friends and acquaintances.

In the workplace it takes on a more formal role but it's still a case of somebody giving feedback and another person being on the receiving end.

When it comes to negative feedback, whether it's to be relayed at home or at work, there's a natural tendency to resist or put off the action because it's concerned with criticism rather than nice, uplifting statements.

In addition we know that we're going to, in many instances, have to put up with defensiveness. Feedback has to be delivered in a way that is regarded as constructive; otherwise it fails in its intention and can cause bad feeling.

Done the right way, you're comparing a person's contribution and behaviour to an expected norm – a certain standard. As such, it is not *personal*. By contrast, if you criticise somebody it's a more personal thing and is usually taken that way.

Constructive feedback focuses on the behaviour of the individual – it's not about the other person's character or their beliefs; it's about what they did.

Note the difference between these two approaches:

'Carla. No chance of *Masterchef* finalist for you. Appreciate you cooking for me and Dad but the meat was like rubber, the vegetables were drowned in that goo of a gravy and the plate just looked a mess.'

'Carla. It's difficult co-ordinating in the kitchen if you're not used to cooking day in, day out. You might like to check the meat with a thermometer next time; perhaps serve the gravy in a boat separately. Appreciate you cooking for us, obviously.'

And between these:

> 'John, people have said your figures are all over the place on the budgeting for this last conference we had. You really ought to be more careful. I know we were under pressure because of the uncertainty about . . . Some of the attendees had trouble getting name badges and were getting quite upset while in line.'

> 'John. I need to discuss the conference. It's difficult; I know we had uncertainty about numbers attending from the overseas offices. The figures were way out. Another time, perhaps you could put two columns in the analysis sheet showing the increased expenditure if we have more people coming. Also a contingency for handwritten badges would be helpful. What do you think about that?'

You can see how the first statements in each case are purely concerned with offering negative feedback. They do nothing to *help* the person improve and certainly nothing to improve their mood. In addition, the statements will invite *defensiveness*.

The second statements leave out any overt criticism and concentrate on the behaviour that you would like to see in the *future* – rather than what occurred. Rather than 'I/we don't like X', it's saying: 'it would be better if you did this as it would result in . . .'. The constructive feedback statement is designed to focus on behaviour that will promote better feelings.

Here's another example:

> 'Nicholas, I don't want you putting the laptop on the dining table when we're eating.'

> 'Nicholas, I'd prefer it if you left your laptop on the desk at dinner time because Dad can then talk to you about next week's drama class.'

The tone in which you deliver statements is also crucial. With any kind of feedback, the paralanguage is especially important. We're programmed to instinctively pick up on the delivery of a message before we assimilate the content.

Thinking of feedback and how people are doing reminds me of a time when I was visiting a client in the USA and I was at his home one early evening.

We were engaged in conversation and his son, Murray (12 years old), strolled in and picked up the phone and made some calls. I could vaguely make out his monosyllabic grunts and short responses to the caller. He seemed to be talking about offering his services for hedge trimming.

His father (my client) looked puzzled as to why his son was speaking in a different voice and kept shaking his head and, with a wry smile, left the room to go to the kitchen for ice for our drinks. I took the opportunity of listening to Murray's next telephone call:

> 'Sir. I'm new to the neighbourhood. I trim hedges. My rates are very competitive. I was walking by your house the other day on the way to school and I noticed you might be needing some assistance soon. Can I do something for you?'

He resumed talking after listening to the person on the other end:

> 'Oh you do . . . Is that so . . .? You're satisfied with him . . . Oh yes, I can see he does a great job. I can see he's very thorough. Not to worry sir, that's ok. I would like to thank you again for your time. Goodbye.'

I was really impressed with Murray's initiative and telephone manner and felt a little sorry for him at the same time.

'Murray', I said, 'I hope you don't feel disheartened after that last call. I'm sure you'll get some work. You handled that call well.'

Turning to me, with a smile on his face, he replied: 'Oh, no need. I already have him as a client. I was just checking – *to see how I was doing!*'

47

Don't forget the 'positives' at work

Too often in the working world – and in life – we focus on telling others what they're doing wrong – rather than what they're doing right. A common complaint is that, in the workplace, managers often don't think to express appreciation and give positive feedback for something done well.

There's a maxim that says, if possible, give positive feedback in public and negative feedback in private. Of course, there will be exceptions with certain people. For example, people of a more introverted nature may be more appreciative if even positive feedback is delivered in private, one on one. Equally, you may wish to point out some negative aspects of someone's behaviour in front of others for a reason, if appropriate.

What is it about giving positive comments to someone that we find uncomfortable?

Positive feedback is much easier to deliver than that of the negative kind. Parents may be well versed in offering positive feedback to children, but as *adults,* especially in our working lives, it's not as readily performed – and opportunities are squandered.

With positive feedback it's best to:

- state *what* the positive behaviour was;
- the *reason* it was successful;
- and then *thank* them.

Here is an example of positive feedback in action:

'I was impressed with the way you placated the customer over that faulty coffee machine. You gave that lady your undivided attention and expressed the right amount of empathy.

Because you didn't interrupt her she was able to feel as though you cared and wanted to know exactly what problems this caused her during her recent social gathering. She was happy to accept an upgraded version at no extra cost.

I feel we maintained our goodwill. Thanks for your efforts on that.'

Everybody needs affirmation from time to time. We like to know how our character strengths are perceived, and it's a boost to our self-esteem.

That being the case, the importance of recognition and affirmation on a continuous basis is something that managers should recognise.

A poll conducted by Gallup in 2009 concluded that managers should use positive feedback more often than negative feedback. Managers who make a habit of dispensing positive feedback throughout the working week had far more motivated employees.

The Gallup poll showed:

- Those receiving positive feedback were 30 times more likely to feel engaged than those receiving no feedback at all.
- Those receiving negative feedback were 20 times more likely to feel engaged than those receiving *no feedback at all.*

When you see something being done right, positive feedback comments can often serve to make sure that the action is repeated. We're so used to looking for things that aren't being done right and then having to give critical comments, it almost becomes an entrenched habit. You should aim to show appreciation if you want to see an action repeated:

> Manager (to member of the team): 'I've noticed that the client schedules for the last month have been ahead of time every week. Well done to you and thanks.'

The person on the receiving end of positive feedback comments is more motivated to continue and repeat their actions. Taking a person's good work for granted without recognising it, and focusing on any minor flaws, is rarely helpful.

Below is a conversation between Diana (a PA) and her boss Mrs. Peel (after she returns from a weekend conference):

> DIANA: 'Mrs. Peel. Did the car go to your house first to pick up your husband and daughters, as I arranged?'
>
> MRS. PEEL: 'Yes, Diana. He then came here and picked me up. It was a good idea of yours to have sandwiches delivered to the house, for our journey. Kept the two girls quiet – they're always hungry. Oh, and I got the Power Point printout you arranged.'
>
> DIANA: 'Well, I felt it might help you in your presentation.'
>
> MRS. PEEL: 'Yes. I don't know how I would have managed without it. Oh – just one thing Diana, while I remember.'
>
> DIANA: 'Yes.'

MRS. PEEL: 'Next time, no mayonnaise.'

DIANA: 'Err . . . OK' (taken aback – as she was expecting a statement of thanks – she regained her composure and getting up from her desk to leave for the day).

DIANA: 'By the way Mrs. Peel. Are you familiar with the famous quote by the French philosopher De La Bruyere?'

MRS. PEEL: 'No.'

She reaches over to her desk drawer, pulls out a piece of paper, hands it to her boss, grabs her coat, smiles and says: 'See you tomorrow morning'. Her boss looks at the piece of paper, which has a quote written on it. Half an hour later she calls Diana on her mobile number:

MRS PEEL: 'Hello Diana. I just wanted to say: "thank you".'

DIANA: 'You're welcome. See you tomorrow.'

Her boss sighs, bites her lip, picks up the piece of paper and decides to pin it on the wall right above her desk. It reads:

There is no excess in the world as commendable as excessive gratitude.

Jean De La Bruyere (1645–1696)

48

'Praise sandwich'

(hold the carbs!)

'The trouble with most of us is that we would rather be ruined by praise than saved by criticisms.'

Norman Vincent Peale

Being human, it's natural that we feel more comfortable receiving positive feedback, but second best we can handle 'constructive feedback' (see #46). It's become more palatable since it replaced the term 'constructive criticism', which seems to be in use less and less (*oh, the power of words!*).

We all want feedback, even if it's not that great. It helps us improve if it's conducted in the right way.

Ayelet Fishbach at the University of Chicago says: '*We're probably unaware that people would like to know how to improve, and they deserve to know. It's their right.*' She believes that the problem lies more with those providing the feedback: '*Negative feedback is often buried and not very specific.*'

The trouble is, in many cases it's often delivered as the dreaded 'praise sandwich' in the working world (sometimes known as the 'feedback sandwich'). Either way, it's not very appetising!

Here's how it goes, if you haven't already come across it. The manager slips the constructive feedback in the *middle*, between two layers of positive feedback or praise (think of this as the 'bread').

So, the three-part conversation goes:

1. positive comments
2. 'constructive' (negative) feedback
3. positive comments.

This means *starting* and *ending* with positive talk, effectively 'sandwiching' the criticism inside the phrase.

The problem with this approach is that, with more and more emphasis on trust in the workplace, many people appreciate a more direct and descriptive statement regarding areas that need working on.

The best managers are also good leaders. They show respect to members of their staff and this, in turn, inspires the staff to do that little bit extra in their work. It also inspires them to seek constructive feedback from the manager – delivered in an honest and empathetic way.

Many younger or inexperienced employees can end up confused with the way the 'praise sandwich' is framed. In addition, when transitioning from the first 'slice' of positive feedback to the middle 'constructive feedback', it quite often entails the use of the word 'but', with its 'discounting effect' (see #20).

In many cases, if the praise is too heavy it can obscure the intended constructive feedback, such that the listener only hears the praise element and the rest of it gets lost:

Praise (1): 'Ken, the open day you organised was well-received by everyone. The Edinburgh folk were grateful you'd thought of pre-ordering taxis back to the station and I also had compliments from others about the evening drinks and nibbles function.'

Criticism (2): 'Before I forget, there are complaints from Manchester and Bristol about you not keeping them well-enough informed about events. They feel they've missed out on attending our last three events.'

Praise (3): 'You've put in a lot of time and effort for the event and I'd like to thank you for all your efforts.'

Combining good and bad news as a sandwich is confusing and often misses the point. Also, the constructive feedback (or criticism) is followed by positive comments. So, in a sense, the positive parts of the message, *which are important to the recipient*, get 'thrown out with the bath water'. The positive element is important for motivational purposes for the employee in such a meeting. The result is that the manager often experiences 'feedback lash' from the person being appraised. They regard the praise as a lead-in to the criticism.

If you have bad news to deliver, or negative feedback, then speak up. Be honest and straight so your listener can hear the real message.

The 'praise sandwich' is only really appropriate when you're having to give negative comments or feedback to someone you don't know or perhaps don't know very well. As you become more acquainted with a person and develop some rapport you can then go into straight-talking mode and cut out the 'bread'.

When research is conducted with managers or superiors as to why they feel the need to use this technique, unsurprisingly they feel that it's easier for people to accept negative comments if it's accompanied by praise. It's a widely held assumption. They believe it shows a 'balanced' assessment.

Now and again the deliverer of the feedback will admit that they use the 'praise sandwich' because they feel uncomfortable delivering negative comments if they can't 'sugar-coat' the conversation with some praise before and after. However, the longer a session goes on, the more discomfort there is for both parties.

Research conducted with recipients of this type of feedback session – from a superior – shows that most people would like to just hear the adverse comments delivered in a competent way.

Some say that it creates a distance between them and their manager because it means they are suspicious of the positive comments given at the beginning and the end, believing that it makes them sound insincere. So it can have a 'boomerang' effect and undermine the message *and* a relationship at the same time.

Saving good things so that they can 'dilute' negative feedback during, for example, a yearly appraisal does nothing to motivate staff for the rest of the year. It's best to deliver either positive or negative feedback nearer the time.

Hope seems to be on the way. The head of Accenture in 2015 announced, in an interview with the *Washington Post,* that they were scrapping the annual job appraisal for their worldwide staff: '*Once a year (I) share with you what I think of you. That doesn't make any sense. People want to know . . . am I doing all right? Nobody's going to wait for an annual cycle to get that feedback.*'

This is a 'U-turn' from a consultancy that has made mind-boggling revenue from helping clients perform these very functions!

If your job function calls for appraising people in a formal way after long intervals, maybe it's time for an alternative. We're in a society of instant feedback in the present day.

Maybe organisations should employ managers who are capable of giving feedback to members of their team all the time – not just annually.

Time and time again employees say they would like to be given positive feedback and comments on a *regular* basis, not necessarily in a 'meeting' but while on the job. It's more motivating and it provides encouragement throughout the year.

49

'Tread softly for you tread
on my dreams . . .'

'I have spread my dreams under your feet. Tread softly because you tread on my dreams.'

W.B. Yeats, *'The Cloths of Heaven'*

We all go through life with dreams. Our own *self-talk* is hugely responsible for how far we get in attaining our goals. We can sometimes sabotage our potential success by our own negative words, as they erode our confidence in achieving our dreams and ambitions.

So we seek support from others in conversation. How they respond to us plays a big part in our level of self-concept. If they encourage us, it gives us motivation.

Yet, often, people mistake the *reason* for a person talking about their concerns or aspirations. They think the person is after a 'solution' – they'll often give reasons or advice (usually based on logic) as to why it won't work or why it might be a waste of time. They think they're helping.

By offering solutions to our 'problems', others impose their own thoughts upon our concerns. Yet often the purpose is not to ask them for their opinions and seek their counsel, but rather to hear yourself working through an episode aloud.

Sometimes people talk because they want to air their thoughts and gain acceptance for their feelings about their aspirations. Most of the time they'll get 'advice' as to what the *drawbacks* are and what it could lead to unless they proceed with caution. These are *logical* reasons, but it's *emotions* that drive our dreams.

It's part of the listening problem: we're so keen to shortcut that we don't listen for meaning 'in between the lines' and just go straight in and offer a *'solution'*.

If you're offering advice or 'solutions', try and distinguish whether the person is seeking an objective opinion or maybe just *moral support* for an idea or aspiration.

Carl Rogers was the founding father of 'person-centred' psychotherapy in the 1940s and 1950s. He coined the term 'reflective listening'. He believed that the answers to the patient's questions were within the patient and not the therapist.

The role of the therapist was to create an environment where the patient could discover the answers themselves. He did this through a willingness to attentively listen without interruption, judgement or giving advice, and a desire to exhibit empathy by understanding and appreciating a client's perspective so that they were able to express their true feelings without fear of judgement.

He believed that by reflecting the person's words in another way, it led to two things. The first was an indicator that the listener was paying attention to what was being said, with an empathic understanding of the speaker's thoughts and feelings. The second outcome was that the speaker heard their own thoughts played back in different words. He noted that many of his clients would tell him that their beliefs and goals felt more real to them when another person presented them back to them. They wanted to hear themselves working through the episode aloud.

We can learn from Rogers' style of listening. Sometimes it's support and affirmation (rather than advice) that is required by another person.

It's natural that if we hear someone making statements or posing a question in a hesitant voice, indicating doubt or fear about pursuing a 'dream', we want to offer an opinion or advice.

If they say:

> 'I'm giving up my job. I'm going to pursue my lifelong dream as a ballet dancer. I loved ballet lessons at school. But I feel guilty about leaving my job and what the future may turn out to be.'

The temptation in this situation is to offer well-meaning advice based on *rational* and economic arguments. Usually, the other person doesn't want to hear statements such as:

> 'You'll have to train for a long time. It will put off your immediate plans for purchasing your own flat. That's a good job in finance that you'll be giving up.'

In the above example a more empathic response along the 'Rogerian' line might be:

> 'It looks as though your lifelong passion is guiding you.'

> 'Yes, I just want to be sure that things work out for the future.'

> 'None of us can ever know that, we often have to go with our driving "gut" feeling.'

> 'Yes, I feel that way.'

> 'You've obviously worked out that you can finance yourself during training and defer plans for a flat till later.'

'Yes, I can share with a friend until I'm ready.'

'Sounds like you're in a perfect situation to make a decision now.'

Quite often we rush to provide a 'fix' to somebody's 'problem', or give our own advice when a person is really looking for a person to listen to them and reflect their thoughts back to them, in a different way, not to 'tread' on their dreams.

I remember giving a motivational workshop a few years ago and there were two ladies on the course who were keen to pursue their own 'dream' but were worried about the time it would take – and also the possibility of failure. They were fearful of taking the plunge and felt they couldn't go through with it. But they didn't want to look back years later and *regret* that they hadn't had the courage.

I've mentioned that songs can be really inspirational and that some songwriters seem to be able to pen words that are just like poetry. I felt it was time to illustrate with some words from my favourite female singer, Karen Carpenter. With that pitch-perfect and poignant voice she often sang about 'dreams'. As she sang: '. . . *the future may say, blame blind yesterday* . . .' (for chasing dreams away).

What an effect this had on the ladies. They seized on the lyrics of *'the future'* blaming *'blind yesterday'*. They were convinced that they shouldn't wait a moment longer. Sheer poetry. The magic of words!

Sometimes a person just wants a sounding board for their ideas, and the act of just being *heard* helps them to do their own soul searching. They want the listener to buy into their dream.

50

'Trust me, I'm a doctor'

'The devil has put a penalty in all things we enjoy in life. Either we suffer in health, or we suffer in soul, or we get fat.'

Albert Einstein

There's much we can learn from experiences with doctors, physicians and health care professionals. Medicine has its own language but, aside from that, there are other communication problems. The following will serve as a reminder of how some of the things that *some* doctors don't do well – on the interpersonal skills front – can remind us how we should strive to deal with people whom we are involved with in our personal and working lives.

How often is your talk littered with words and jargon that cause confusion?

And how intuitive are you in picking up the 'listening' body language that signifies this, in your interaction with others?

A report by the Royal College of GPs (RCGP) in 2014 asked doctors, in their interactions with patients, to:

- speak more slowly
- use plain English
- cut out too much jargon.

The NHS's annual survey of more than 64,500 hospital patients showed that 24 per cent felt as though the doctors sometimes *talked over* them as if they didn't exist. Furthermore, 20 per cent felt there was a trust issue in that they didn't feel they had confidence in the doctors. More than a third couldn't always *understand* what they were being told.

Doctors have a reputation for being poor listeners. Much of this is related to eye contact. When it is present it promotes the feeling of confidence and honesty on the part of the physician and promotes trust. It helps to reinforce or contradict their verbal comments.

When they are saying something to a patient – and when a patient is saying something to them – they may well not be looking at the patient. A screen or paperwork may be their object of attention. They may be too busy writing down what the person is saying rather than giving them attention. For the patient, the perception is that they are not listening.

One of the studies reported in the *British Journal of General Practice* (2010) cited that it was the doctor's tone of voice and lack of eye contact that patients interpreted as a sign that their doctor seemed uninterested in them. They also did not believe a reassuring verbal comment if it was accompanied by *contradictory* facial expressions and vocal hesitancy.

The increasing use of computers has resulted in practitioners *looking* less at the patient, *saying* less and asking fewer *questions*. The result is that with the patient having limited opportunity to voice their concerns and volunteer information, the doctor may miss or forget information.

The studies suggest that patients should speak up: 'If you're unhappy there are polite ways to speak up. Patients should feel empowered to say "I didn't understand your language that you used. Can you explain it in laymen's terms?" You can tell your doctor if you feel rushed or anxious. Don't worry about offending the doctor – if patients don't speak up they may not realise there's a problem.'

Much of the time, doctors routinely talk to patients using medical terms and acronyms that mean nothing to their listeners and can cause misunderstandings. The situation is made worse by the fact that most patients hearing the 'gobbledygook' *pretend* they understand what's being told to them.

Studies show, unsurprisingly, that patients make poor health-related choices if they're confused by the medical jargon that they hear while in the presence of the doctor. Doctors are often unaware that they're using jargon (through force of habit) and often – if they're looking at a screen or paperwork – don't pick up from a patient's facial expression that they're confused or that they might like some clarification.

In the USA the Joint Commission, the group that accredits hospitals, sent out a directive requiring doctors to cut out overly technical language and '*to communicate in a manner that meets the patient's oral and written communication needs*'.

The use of 'medicalese' as a language causes problems on both sides of the Atlantic. Some doctors, for example, cite how a misunderstanding occurs with just the use of the word '*diet*'. They say that, for them, it means 'food', but patients think it means they are suggesting they 'go on a diet'. Another word is 'exercise', where the doctors are trying to encourage 'walking' but some patients think it means 'going to the gym'.

As long as patients don't ask questions or indicate that they haven't understood what the doctor or health care worker has said, there will be problems. Through feeling intimidated, being in a state of anxiety or not wanting to look stupid, patients put their health and progress at risk when they don't understand what the doctor has told them.

Patients often say that if they do pluck up the courage to ask questions, the answers come back full of *more* jargon!

We know that a creeping use of jargon is to be found in most professions (see #42). But the difference is that when used in the medical profession, it can be life-threatening.

The doctor's communication with the patient should be different from their conversations with their fellow medical professionals. While it acts as a *shorthand* for them, it often baffles the patient.

One lady told me how she left a doctor's surgery many years ago feeling really deflated as the parting words by the doctor – after she asked if she was 'silly' bothering him about her symptoms – were: 'It's idiopathic'.

Having never come across this jargon before, she had the voice in her head telling her that her doctor believed she was an 'idiot'!

It was only later, when she discussed it with her partner, that his enquiries assured her that it was a medical term that doctors use when they don't know the cause of a patient's symptoms or condition.

The RCGP report, mentioned earlier, cites the words 'chronic' and 'positive' as examples of doctors using words with patients and not realising that the meaning is often unclear:

For doctors – 'chronic' means persistent or long term.

For patients – 'chronic' means severe (with all the associated confusion and worry).

For doctors: tests that prove 'positive' may signify bad news.

For patients: tests that prove 'positive' are wrongly assumed to be good news.

As one doctor commented while addressing the problem, health care professionals must become 'medically bilingual'. In other words, they must learn to speak 'medicalese' *and* plain language.

A doctor's ability to explain, listen and empathise has a profound impact on a patient's care. A *New York Times* article (2015) perhaps sums up the problem, with the headline 'Doctor, Shut Up and Listen'.

It cited reports by the Joint Commission, which revealed that 'communication failure' (as opposed to lack of technical skills) was responsible for over 70 per cent of adverse health outcomes in hospitals. A further disturbing finding was that, on average, the doctor waited just 18 seconds before *interrupting* a patient who was detailing their concerns and symptoms! Brief and rushed encounters were common.

Another study revealed that in more than 60 per cent of cases the patient *misunderstood* instructions after leaving the doctor's surgery.

This humorous tale illustrates the point. A man went to see his doctor after gaining a lot of weight through attending work functions:

'I can sum up my advice in four words' the doctor said, writing it down and then handing the piece of paper to his patient. (No eye contact.)

'Don't eat anything fatty', the patient read out from the piece of paper.

The doctor rose from his seat to usher his patient out of the door.

'You mean – no cheese, butter or chocolate?' the patient enquired.

The GP looked at the note he'd just handed to him and shaking his head replied: 'Oh, I missed out a comma after the third word.'

51

'Trust me, err . . . I'm, err . . . a politician'

'Political language is designed to make lies sound truthful, and to give an appearance of solidity to wind.'
George Orwell, 'Politics and the English Language' (1946)

W as George Orwell right? In other words, are politicians giving us an idea of how *not* to communicate?
The gripes that we have relating to some of the techniques, speech patterns and use of words used in the world of politics can help us know what to avoid when we are conversing in our own lives – if we want to further relationships and inspire trust.

We see the dark arts of political obfuscation every day in government announcements. We can study the way that some politicians operate as a lesson for our own way of communicating.

Rhetoric is an ancient tradition and its origins go back centuries. It was highly revered as a noble method of 'persuasion', but in the present day all too often we tend to align it with politicians and spin-doctors. In fact, you'll often hear the word 'empty' before it.

Politicians are most often connected with spin-doctors. We recognise this as an element of PR associated with psychological manipulation. It's used to create a message or to cover up something, and may involve denial or other methods to distract the public and create a diversion.

When people talk about politicians now, they'll invariably mention 'doublespeak' – language that deliberately disguises, distorts or reverses the meaning of words. It may take the form of *euphemisms,* making truth less unpleasant without denying its nature. As Quentin Crisp commented: *'Like secret agents on a delicate mission . . . euphemisms are unpleasant truths wearing diplomatic cologne.'*

We also associate 'weasel words' with politicians. It was Theodore Roosevelt who brought the term to wide attention when in a speech he said: *'One of our defects as a nation is a tendency to use what have been called weasel words. When a weasel sucks eggs the meat is sucked out of the egg. If you use a weasel word after another there is nothing left of the other.'*

You'll hear variations of phrases like these all the time: 'This is clearly correct'; 'I'm reasonably confident that . . .'; 'Nearly all of the people I talk to on the doorsteps tell me . . .'; and 'Let me be clear about this.'

George Orwell believed that politicians' language was necessarily vague or meaningless because it was intended to *hide* the truth rather than express it. Do you find yourself communicating in this way? Political commentators say that the powers that be always like to give the impression that they're knowledgeable and in control, but in truth – they don't know.

If we observe them in interviews we often see them having to choose their words carefully as they respond with: '*I'm glad you brought up that point.*' Or another favourite: '*That's a good question.*'

(As someone once said: 'When someone says, "that's a good question", you can be sure it's a lot better than the answer you're going to get.')

I once heard a politician say to an interviewer: '*I'll just rephrase your question before I answer it.*' (Who's asking the questions?!)

Of course, most political interviewers and observers are used to politicians avoiding giving an answer to a question. This is something we can learn from in our own dealings with people. We know how frustrating it is to listen to the politician who is asked an awkward question that shows them or their party in a negative light. They may answer the question with a *question,* or try and focus on something that relates to the point on which a positive 'spin' can be applied.

The spin words and phrases are often designed to appeal to our emotions – love of country, desire for peace, freedom – designed to make scrutiny of the idea itself secondary.

We know that politicians in general do not like to admit they are wrong and therefore it is rare to hear them say sorry for their gaffes. Some are masters of the 'non-apology' apology (**see #32**). On the rare occasion that they appear to be doing so, you could come away feeling a little perplexed.

Here's a good example: in 2015 the leader of the Labour Party was criticised for posing with *The Sun* newspaper for a PR stunt and was then forced into making an apology. In a radio interview the deputy leader, Harriet Harman, told the LBC radio presenter that the leader was 'right' to apologise for posing with the newspaper, but was also 'right' to have posed for it in the first place.

(What was that all about?! Obfuscation, doublespeak or what?)

Yet, occasionally we'll come across politicians who possess that 'likeability' factor and some of the sins are forgiven – or, rather, put on hold for a time. Ronald Reagan was initially written off as a simpleton who wouldn't be able to cut it – they were fond of saying 'he owned more horses than books'. Despite one congressman saying '*You can walk through his deepest thoughts without getting your feet wet*' it didn't hurt his reputation. He was a great Republican success story. Now all presidents want to be as uninformed as he was. His secret weapon? Plain speaking.

Margaret Thatcher became more famous on the world stage than any British prime minister, except for Sir Winston Churchill. She too achieved much of her success through straight talk – both formally and informally.

Charles Moore's authorised biography (2015) of the 'Iron Lady' describes the historic meeting in 1984 between Mrs Thatcher and Mikhail Gorbachev at Chequers to discuss the SDI – popularly known as the 'Star Wars' initiative.

'It produced almost nothing but disagreement, and the sharpness in tone exceeded all the usual Foreign Office euphemisms for rude and quarrelsome meetings, such as "frank" or "candid".' Yet it was hailed a success as Gorbachev – who dashed off because he was nearly two hours late for his reception at the Soviet Embassy – parted by saying their dialogue should continue as he agreed with her about 'the value of talking'.

Mrs Thatcher's successful straight talking continued – as the biography describes – for after briefly lingering with her officials she exclaimed: '*Tomorrow it's China, and I haven't had my hair done!*' She ran upstairs and was gone.

Today we're more used to politician soundbites:

'It's good for the economy.'

'A Budget for strivers, drinkers and drivers.'

'Good for jobs.'

'We're all in it together.'

Andrew Marr, while interviewing a politician on his BBC politics show (November 2015), noted the mention of '*hard-working families*' a total of six times and finished his interview with an exasperated request: '*I am going to make a plea to you and all Conservative politicians as well. Could we please stop saying "hard-working families" quite so often?*'

Apart from soundbites, from time to time we have to endure the occasional 'malapropism', from an American president perhaps: '*It will take time to restore chaos and order.*' or '*The French don't have a word for entrepreneur.*'!

There are a number of techniques often used by our political masters to manipulate public opinion. Are you guilty of any of the following?:

- denial is a common one (deny anything first, then come back with an explanation)
- create a diversion – then publicise the distraction (good or bad) to divert attention away from what needs to be covered up
- quote statistics that are out of context, which misleads the public (numbers are an easy option to use to reframe an argument)
- feign indignance (of the 'how dare you' variety)
- make a personal attack on an opponent instead of responding to a question or argument
- cite information to support an argument from an 'expert opinion' – but this can be misleading
- fear may be generated with the electorate, and then the spin-doctors get to work by providing solutions
- a technique called the 'false choice', which is beloved of politicians – essentially one of two options is offered – an either/or – there's no middle way
- adopt the 'common man' approach, which involves copying the manner and style of the particular audience. Sometimes they may adopt the accent of the local audience and use similar idioms. It can backfire and antagonise an audience (see the example below).

The Chancellor George Osborne was visiting a supermarket distribution centre in 2013. He seemed to have ditched his previous RP (received pronunciation) accent on that day, when he gave a speech to the warehouse workers – and the press was quick to seize on the transformation, as they reported: British became '*Briddish*', 'want to' was '*wanna*', want it became '*wannit*' and 'we have had as '*we've 'ad a*'. Osborne added: '*We're buildin' a benefits system that means ya always bedda off in work.*'

You're exposed to politicians' messages every day. Become aware of the irritants that have an effect on you and erode your trust. Make sure that you converse in a manner that is sincere.

We've become increasingly distrustful of politicians. We don't even trust election results now. Just *rearrange* the words:

ELECTION RESULTS. What do we get?

LIES – LET'S RECOUNT (!)

The lexicon of politician-speak can help us to realise how trust can be eroded when plain speaking is avoided.

Be aware of your linguistic 'style' when you converse with others. *Let me be clear about this!*

52

'I want to tell you a story . . .'

'After nourishment, shelter and companionship, stories are the thing we need most in the world.'

Philip Pullman

We are all storytelling machines. From a neurological point of view, our brain structure is extremely receptive to narratives. Research shows how strongly a story can tap into our emotions and release neurotransmitters that promote understanding and encourage us to take action.

Have you ever been in a gathering or lecture or meeting, closely reaching your boredom threshold and then suddenly you hear the words, '*I want to tell you a story*'? Immediately you perk up and the speaker has your attention. It starts from childhood with our fascination for fairy tales, myths and parables. Some of these have been passed down for not just hundreds but thousands of years.

A study was carried out at Stanford Graduate School of Business in which students were asked to give a one-minute pitch. Just one in ten students was asked to use a story within the pitch. The others were asked to go for the more traditional elements of *facts* and *figures*. The class then had to write down everything they remembered about each pitch:

- 5 per cent of students cited a statistic
- 63 per cent remembered the story.

Their research concluded that 'Our brains are not hard-wired to understand logic or retain facts for very long. Our brains are wired to understand and retain stories.'

They went on to say: 'A story is a journey that moves the listener, and when the listener goes on that journey they feel different and the result is persuasion and sometimes action.'

So is it just emotions that we're trying to tap? Does that mean facts and figures are not that important?

'No one says facts and figures should be completely eliminated from your storytelling', the Stanford researchers report. 'When data and story are used *together*, audiences are moved both emotionally and intellectually.'

The problem with numbers is that because they are abstract they don't stick in people's memories. Stories are good for capturing listeners' attention and helping them to relate to the topic you're discussing. And they tend to be remembered.

Researchers Mazzocco and Green (Ohio State University/University of North Carolina) arc experts in narrative persuasion and they conducted extensive research in legal settings ('What's the Story?' Vol 23, May 2011).

Their findings were that the opinions and beliefs that people hold are primarily *emotional* in nature. Research shows that it is often difficult to influence attitudes that are emotion-driven by using rationalistic, rhetorical arguments.

They point out something that has been backed by many previous studies – that stories are far more *influential* than facts. A story has the capacity to alter our emotional beliefs in a way that 'logic' can't. Give the story a beginning, a middle and an end. And make sure the paralinguistics are right. Use pauses to reinforce, and also pacing and emphasis.

Stories are a great attention-holder and promote better understanding, whether you're talking one on one or to many people. Just think of a wedding, for example. How much time, anxiety and sweat are expended by the 'best man' as he strives to create the perfect story to regale the audience? It's usually stories that keep the guests entertained and attention-focused during the speech (even through a haze of alcohol!). We tend to engage better if somebody starts to tell us a story. Remember the excitement of childhood, which was largely predicated on stories?

Stories enable you to bring up a number of points in an understandable way and in a short space of time. Your listener(s) may identify with what you have conveyed from their own experiences and this is great for building rapport.

There's another priceless benefit about relaying a story as – since it comes from memory – you are able to relay it fluently and it makes you come across as a fluent speaker. If the story relates to something that happened to you in your working and/or personal life, the listeners are able to learn more about you and your values.

If you're giving a presentation then a story is ideal as it helps allay nerves and fear of forgetting. You know the story inside out so you're able to devote more time to looking at the audience, making eye contact instead of looking down at notes or looking away to a screen with slides.

The stories can be personal – showing how you encountered a problem, what it caused and how you solved it – the classic beginning, middle and end. Being personal it helps you connect with your audience and makes it memorable as people can identify with it in a 'this happened to me too' way.

Or a story can be business-related. The format of the story can be simple. For example: 'a client contacted us about X; we suggested Y; we completed the project by doing it this way and they were really satisfied; they've now asked us if we can help them with Z'.

So let's recap and look at some of the advantages of using a story, whether it's in a meeting, speaking publicly or having a personal conversation:

- It's simply the best way to hold your audience's *attention*.
- It helps you to *illustrate* your point – it usually involves people, a problem and a triumph.
- Everyone loves a good story. If you're making a speech you're more likely to *connect* with your audience if you tell a true story involving real characters.
- You'll become more relaxed in a *formal* speech situation as you'll know your story – therefore you won't need any notes.
- Most people will forget *facts* and *figures*, but they always tend to remember a good story.

Let me tell *you* a story now.

Not all mistakes end in failure – we can learn from them and become better (given the chance!). It's a story about IBM from the 1960s.

A manager made a decision that lost the company $10 million. He was summoned to the office of the CEO, Tom Watson. When asked why he'd been called there, the manager said: '*So you can fire me?*' Watson replied, '*Fire you? Of course I'm not going to fire you. I've just spent $10 million educating you.*'

Disagree without being *disagreeable*

'Diplomacy is the art of letting somebody else have your way.'
David Frost

We can't avoid disagreement. In our domestic life every day produces a bundle of new disagreements. In the workplace it's essential. Why? How else are new and better ideas born? Companies that don't have a culture of allowing employees the opportunity to present alternative views lose out in all ways.

I've spent time over the years in meetings, with a degree of awe at how some people are able to manage to show disagreement at somebody's comments or ideas in a way that *invites* disharmony. Meetings have been wrecked by the unnecessary way in which a person has voiced disagreement.

Just to highlight my point, take this simple statement of disagreement to someone present at a meeting: 'That's not a good idea.'

Apart from the obvious ego defence, that person may have spent days or weeks coming up with this 'treasure'! And now, to be told in front of others that it's not a good idea by one of your peers . . . (If it's a boss telling you that, it's even worse.)

Suppose we expressed it in this alternative way: 'There are some things that bother me about this idea . . .'?

You can see that the discussion will take a new direction and, more importantly, you're preserving the 'status' of the person that has voiced the idea. *You're disagreeing without being disagreeable.*

I watched close to a year's output of BBC Two's *Newsnight* and observed the actions and body language of people after being told by one or more of the other guests – 'I disagree with you', or words in that vein such as 'you're wrong' or 'you're talking rubbish'.

Inevitably, the non-verbal signals from some guests were very telling as they tried to conceal their irritation. The guests that felt confident in 'defending' their point of view invariably spoke in a level tone with careful word choice.

The politicians, or whoever it was forced to be on the 'defensive' in response to the statement of disagreement levelled at them, almost always came out in a negative light. Their voice-pitch changed as they tried to *suppress* emotions and their word choice and delivery invited interruption and counter-attack.

Why would you want to tell somebody you disagree with them using the word 'disagree' when it's one of those words that goes straight to the ego? That person then becomes focused on another objective: how to disagree with YOU!

It invites defensiveness and shuts down effective listening from them as their brain goes into overdrive and prepares for a suitable riposte. So a lot of your reasons for disagreement are not even *heard* – even though your points may be helpful and valid.

The secret of more cordial interactions is to try and indicate your disagreement with phrases that essentially say the *same* thing but don't turn the interlude into an adversarial encounter. There are many variations on the following:

- 'I see it a different way.'
- 'The information I've been given conflicts with your explanation . . .'
- 'I find it difficult to follow that line of thinking . . .'
- 'I agree with your points about . . . it's the effect on X that concerns me.'

If you're talking face-to-face with someone then this will at least keep the 'turn-taking' of conversation close to normal. If it's an interview on the TV or radio then the interviewer usually allows each person to respond in turn.

As we've discussed earlier, people need to feel they have been listened to. Use the paraphrasing technique to show that you've heard them. Use good questioning to lead them through your confusion or reservations. But make the questions such that they can be taken only in a *positive* way:

> 'Simon, I get the logic of what you're saying. Can you just explain about the need for moving X section out from the main building and over to Shuttleworth? Will finance then find that they have to outsource some of their activities?'

When you respond in a way that shows concern rather than disagreement, it leads to the concerns being satisfied or an indication that the ideas need to be thought through more. But it's all done in a conciliatory way.

Remember, at all times, that disagreements usually fall into two categories:

- either they're task-related
- or they're people-related.

If your resistance is because of a personal nature, to do with people, then it is usually more difficult to advance your cause. Inevitably, the discussions become adversarial and logic gives way to emotion.

I frequently witness conversations, in or out of meetings, where the whole thing breaks down because any initial differing point of view becomes compounded due to people choosing to exaggerate while disagreeing:

'If we change the furnishings, Jeremy, we'll end up bankrupt.'

'No, Grace, reallocating our resources from security to staff kitchen means we'll have break-ins all the time . . .'

The focus then switches to the defence of a knee-jerk exaggeration rather than the *original* point.

There's a technique that's highly effective in domestic or professional settings, which leads to less 'disagreement' dialogue – the switch to 'suggesting'. Take the idea and pose it as a question. It invites less resistance as everybody sees an invitation to contribute. Consider this:

'How about we all go and try the new Ferris wheel this afternoon instead of the cinema, when you're back from school?'

'How about if we introduced a flexitime approach for two weeks of the month?'

The paralanguage is very important, as you would expect, when you're disagreeing. The tone should suggest cooperation not hostility. You want the perception to be one of solution-searching on your part. If you listen to radio and TV interviews with one or more guests you'll hear adversarial talk that changes the tenor of the interviews:

'You don't know what you're talking about.'

'Hang on, I haven't finished.'

'If you'll be quiet for a moment, I'll answer your question.'

Whereas a non-confrontational tone with neutral language that minimises defensiveness allows you to probe further into the reasons for another person's viewpoint:

'It's intriguing that you consider a health club should be top of the list in any refurbishment budget. Is there some evidence for this?'

You're showing respect for a person's contribution, even though you disagree with his or her comments, and it opens up the discussion and may naturally expose any weaknesses.

We've discussed feelings earlier on. If you're a manager, for example, and you hear a 'feeling statement' (to do with emotion), rather than ride roughshod over people's feelings (which will get you nowhere) *consider agreeing with how they might feel*. So, for example, you might say:

> 'Emma, I can fully appreciate that, in your eyes, his actions came across as uncaring and arrogant . . .'

> 'I can understand that moving over to this new position – to avoid redundancy – might make you feel cut off from all the people you've worked with over the years . . .'

Be aware that we all have different points of view and that when your viewpoint differs with others the idea is not to prove them wrong, but to open up a discussion – in a conciliatory way.

54

Giving and receiving praise

'I can live for two months on a good compliment.'

Mark Twain

How often do you find yourself praising someone? Your spouse, children, friends, work colleagues? How much are you on the receiving end of praise – in your private and working life? We're all potentially giving and receiving praise.

Yet many of us have trouble accepting praise as well as giving it – and knowing how to deliver it effectively. Many people treat praise with the same unease as critical comments. They think it's going to be followed by some criticism. Small wonder, since many parents and managers in companies are fond of using the 'praise sandwich' when wanting to deliver negative messages (**see #48**).

Studies have shown that it is in the working environment where the least amount of praise is given. In one study, 70 per cent of employees said they would have a more positive attitude about themselves if the boss was inclined to show gratitude through praise, and 81 per cent said that they would work harder.

Why is gratitude scarce at work? Quite often the managers are *untrained* and *inexperienced* and consequently don't understand the power of reinforcement from sincere praise.

There's a self-perpetuating situation that exists when managers don't receive praise or recognition from *their* boss, and so the culture never develops. They don't get praise – so you don't get praise. Being preoccupied with everyday activities can also make this a low priority for managers.

For some people, the idea of praising somebody's performance is completely out of character. To do its job, praise has to be *authentic*. People can be suspicious of praise and fear manipulation of some sort is in the offing. We're used to the put-down more than praise (especially if the giver has an audience!). So it has to be *sincere* for it to be believable.

There's no question that, from an interpersonal point of view, looking out for praiseworthy actions in social and business life makes for better relationships. You will often be remembered for the comments that you gave about what someone did, what they said or their appearance.

In order for your delivery of praise to be effective – and to help people believe the sincerity of your comments – it's best to be *specific* with the praise. Compare these pairs of statements and consider which is more effective:

'Good keynote speech you gave yesterday.' Or: 'I really enjoyed your speech yesterday – your bit about hearing and listening was really eye-opening. I'm practising already.'

'That was a wonderful dinner party'. Or: 'We really enjoyed the dinner party. To get two lovely courses made like that – with no hitches – I don't know how you do it.'

The point about giving praise that is specific is that the recipient trusts its authenticity. You're believable and they feel genuine appreciation. It's more powerful in its impact. It also helps a person to improve and provides positive feedback.

In the workplace it is particularly important to regularly notice something that merits sincere praise as it is a big motivator and encourages people to give their best. In many organisations praise is often only given – and noticed – for the *big* things: 'Rachel, congratulations on picking up our "PA of the Year" distinction.' People will be used to getting praise and appreciation for this type of thing.

It's the *small* things that are noticed the rest of the time – and commented upon – that give the most satisfaction: 'Judith, I need to let you know this. The reception area always looks inviting and tidy since you joined the company. Well done and thanks.'

However, you can overdo the praise sometimes and not achieve the effect of the sincere appreciation you wish to convey: 'Thanks Tom. You're the best maintenance man in the City, I would say.'

Of course, the recipient of the compliment, Tom, is well aware that this is the judgement of a single person and that there are, no doubt, an infinite number of highly capable office maintenance workers working in the City of London!

Far better for Tom to hear: 'You know, it's comforting having you around Tom, because you're there for a problem almost immediately – and there's usually a good result'. That might have more resonance as it is quite believable and would probably encourage even more good work.

Be careful about giving praise in public to a person while in the company of others who are not being complimented. I've seen (and you have too, no doubt) situations where a person is praised for something and it leaves the other people thinking 'what's wrong with *my dress/ my tie/the presentation I gave/my dog/spectacles/high heels/the apple pie I made*'! It can cause unnecessary bad feeling.

Result: the person given the compliment would rather not have had your words of admiration, as they feel embarrassed for the other people present.

As far as accepting praise is concerned, many people do not feel comfortable *accepting* a compliment and struggle with the words of their reply. There seems to be the feeling that the only way to respond to an appreciative remark or compliment is to *deny* it.

Psycholinguists have observed three responses to a compliment:

1. acceptance
2. deflection
3. rejection.

In the case of the second response option, instead of accepting the praise or rejecting it completely, the person chooses to dilute or deflect the kind words that have been offered:

'Oh, it's just a little something I threw on – had it for ages, falling to bits.'

'Don't know about that. It's just one of those 15-minute Jamie Oliver recipes – pastry was a bit hard.'

'Thanks, but I thought I went on too long in the presentation about the growth projections. Boring.'

There's a comedy sketch by the Emmy award-winning Amy Schumer where a crowd of women come together and throw praise at each other:

'Congratulations on your big promotion.'

'Love your hat.'

'Well, look at your cute *little* dress!' (To which the self-deprecating reply is: 'Little? I'm like a size 100 now. I paid like $2 for it. I look like a whore who got locked out of her apartment.')

At the end of the sketch one of the women in the crowd replies with a single 'thank you' to the compliment she is given, leaving all the other women perplexed!

If you think about it carefully, what you are doing to the compliment-giver, when rejecting their words, is lobbing the ball back over the net with a doubt over their *judgement,* thus ruining the goodwill and making the person giving you the compliment feel rejected.

To make matters worse, what you often witness during these typical responses is the person *interrupting* the praise-giver. *They don't even get the chance to complete their full line of praise before the denial occurs!*

There's a simple way of responding to a compliment. *Accept it.*

Also, while accepting it, *make the other person feel good too.* How about:

'That's nice of you to let me know.'

'That's very kind of you.'

'Thanks. I enjoyed the presentation too.'

'It was a first time and I'm glad it worked.'

'It's good to hear that.'

Or, as the seasoned film and TV celebrities quite often do when paid a compliment by their chat-show host or interviewer, there's always the simple, confident and effective two-word response: 'Thank you'.

Men and women at work

('report' or 'rapport'?)

Extensive research has been conducted, mainly over the last 25 years, into communication between the sexes in the workplace and, in many cases, the effects of two different linguistic styles.

Deborah Tannen, a sociolinguist from Georgetown University, Washington DC, is an expert in the field and her research findings conducted in workplace settings showed that, in most instances:

- women may use words to 'connect' and to express feelings or build *rapport*
- men's talk is often about sharing facts and figures, as in a *report*.

This same reasoning might explain why men and women often handle situations of conflict differently. Women may avoid conflict to maintain closeness (rapport), whereas men may use conflict in order to gain status.

Talking to USA Today (March 11, 2014), Tannen explained why this may be the case: 'Research on children at play holds a clue. Girls tend to use language to maintain and negotiate closeness . . . Boys tend to negotiate their status in the group – who's up, who's down . . .'

She says that this is why, when girls and boys become women and men, those same ways of talking may carry over in the workplace.

Her research recently extended to asking high-ranking men and women to record everything they said for a week, and she then shadowed them and their co-workers. She found that women in authority – more often than men in similar positions – used language in ways that were similar to what the researchers observed among girls when they were engaged in playing together.

Instead of saying 'do this' some women managers would say 'let's' or 'what you could do', or they would 'soften' the impact by making statements sound like questions.

She concludes that women are in somewhat of a double bind at work – if they talk in this fashion *'which is associated with and expected of women, they seem to lack confidence . . .'*. But if they talk in ways expected of someone in authority *'they are seen as too aggressive'*.

Some men find it strange to witness the behaviour of females – either one to one or in a group – discussing a topic of contention. They may witness people who are at ease with one another talking in a disjointed way with interruptions, overlapping of statements and finishing each other's sentences – all done in a perfectly *natural* way and with no bad feeling.

A man may see this as an ineffective way of discussing something, with all the interrupting and sentence-finishing before the other person has finished making their point.

In actual fact, they're witnessing 'rapport talk': *listening for feelings as well as facts.*

Some men may look at the female's line of reasoning and challenge it with facts and figures. Of course, women want a discussion, but all of a sudden it's turning into a debate. They're getting 'report talk'.

You'll hear people suggest that the 'paralanguage' for women should change – that they should emulate men's voices. A recent study, in which ten prominent women business leaders were analysed, showed that, in fact, their voices were closer in pitch to the *average* of all women.

It showed that it's not necessary to go 'male' and try to speak in an unnaturally deep voice. The 'power' for women is denoted by their 'vocal energy' – the *variations* in loudness they use to convey their message – the studies show. It revealed that an *energetic* voice makes women sound authentic and inspires trust.

So women shouldn't have to worry about suppressing their natural expressive behaviour by lowering the pitch of their voice – or by smiling less.

Smiling less? Who's asked for that? Unfortunately, it comes up now and again.

Sarah Sands, who has wide experience in the world of national newspapers and is now the editor of the *London Evening Standard*, has been making a mental note of how much women colleagues smile compared with male ones. She found that women passing each other in the office are far more likely to smile, and that most women smile as they talk.

She says in her article ('Are women being held back by too much smiling?' *Evening Standard*, March 2015):

> *'An expression of women's professional weakness turns out to be the smile. Women smile too easily and often. It becomes expected of them. A senior lawyer at the session remembered a man turning to her at the end of a meeting and asking her why she was not smiling.*
>
> *She replied: "Why should I be smiling? None of the men are smiling." He apologised . . . Women usually prefer to have one to-one conversations rather than public speaking. I know I do. It is also a*

*fact that women smile because it engages others and puts them at
their ease. I should be sorry to see the smile sacrificed as the price
for getting women on boards . . . But while women are held back
for differences, we will just have to play hardball.'*

What about the issue of 'likeability' in the working world? Sheryl Sand-
berg, COO of Facebook, has a definite view on this. She says that the
higher up the corporate ladder the woman goes, the less likeable she
may become. But in the case of men, she argues, the opposite is true:
*'Success and likeability are positively correlated for men and negatively
correlated for women.'*

She finds that, in so many instances, where men would be described
as 'decisive' or leadership material, women may be labelled 'bossy' –
her point being that its use seems to be solely the preserve of powerful
women, and also with a negative connotation. The word 'bossy' is not
the problem, as she says: *'Other words would take its place . . .'*

The last word goes to Deborah Tannen, who said in 2014: 'Let's
agree to stop sending girls and women the message they'll be disliked
if they exercise authority.'

Her point: the notion that power is a male prerogative.

So can and should men try to establish more rapport when dealing
with both males and females; and should women try and converse with
males and females with an objective of status, and converse in a purely
factual way?

The answer, of course, is that we should recognise the *strengths* of
both styles; and be more aware of making sure we use both, as and
when appropriate.

'He said', 'She said' . . .
(just different?)

'This revolution was bound to come. That women are the same as men. But I don't think women are the same as men. How are we different? I feel that we think differently, achieve things by different methods. I think women like chitter-chattering together and I don't think men do. I think men like board meetings and I am not sure women love them quite so much . . .'

Joanna Lumley, *The Times (19 April 2014)*

Let's accept that males and females differ in the way that they think, feel, act and talk. Even the subjects they talk about are typically different. The surveys show that men talk about money, sports and business; women tend to talk about people, relationships and feelings.

It would be very hard to dispute the fact that when speaking to our spouse, partner, family and close friends the talking experiences are totally different to the way that we speak in our working environment. Why? Well, at work we're inevitably adopting a 'role' and therefore that carries with it a more formal linguistic style.

As we discussed earlier, studies show that in general the male 'style' is to display confidence, with a 'one-up' position, while the female's may be more modest with a 'one-down' style that's aiming for connection.

Women 'nag' but men make 'requests'. What's behind this stereotype? It exaggerates whatever differences there are between men and women. By not fitting men's speech patterns, women's language becomes deficient!

With family and friends there's a certain amount of 'taking for granted' that inevitably goes on. Because of that, we often communicate with less thought.

As Claudius says in Shakespeare's *Hamlet*:

'My words fly up, my thoughts remain below, words without thoughts never to heaven go.'

What about the differences in listening? It's said that men don't exhibit the same kind of listening attentiveness that women do. Research into the listening behaviour of girls and women shows that they face each other and maintain good eye contact. When observing boys' and men's behaviour it shows that, in many cases, they have a preference for sitting at *angles* to the person and maintaining a gaze straight ahead, with occasional head-turning to the side towards the person who is speaking.

If you ask most females how they feel about a man listening to her in that position, the response is the same: they don't *feel* the person is listening to them (regardless of whether the person *is* actually listening).

The situation becomes more frustrating because women say that a lot of men are not in the habit of giving '*back channels*' while listening.

Women tend to give a lot of these, such as: 'Oh really?', 'No', 'Right' and 'Never'. The absence of this kind of *interjection* in men means that the speaker doesn't feel confident that the other person is interested in what they're saying, or is even paying attention.

This comment from a relationship psychotherapist is revealing: '. . . During that time I was introduced to a lot of men who had been single for a long time. But nobody could figure out why. Often it was because they put up invisible barriers to women – avoiding eye contact, not smiling, appearing uninterested, not asking open questions.'

Traditionally 'feminine', softer skills – such as sensitivity, empathy, openness and a collaborative rather than a competitive approach – are now seen as skills that are transferable to the workplace and *essential* for commercial success. And these skills are not soft. They're *strong*.

Again, it's language that is distorting the actions. By calling them 'feminine' it can act as a deterrent for some men to want to develop them in favour of the more accepted masculine traits – either in the workplace or at home.

It's been reported that divorce lawyers cite 'he doesn't talk to me' or 'he doesn't listen to me' as the two most common reasons they are approached to handle matrimonial breakdowns. Eyes that first met over the cross-trainer are increasingly now meeting across divorce papers.

So some things will continue to baffle both of the sexes about each other.

Men claim they will just never understand certain things about women, such as:

- Why can't she speak in a more direct way when *requesting* something?
- Why she didn't just *order* chips, if she *wanted* chips ('*these are my chips!*')?

Women claim there are things they will just never understand about men, such as:

- Why can't he have a conversation without it becoming a *debate* (not everything needs to be turned into a competition)?
- Why does he talk all the way through *Strictly Come Dancing* and 'shush' me when *Top Gear* comes on?

The situation with men and women talking to each other in their own distinctive way will continue. But with more emotional intelligence and self-awareness and an acknowledgement that there *are* differences – life can be better.

'*Do you expect me to talk?*'
'*No Mr Bond, I expect you to die.*'

(*James Bond*/Sean Connery
Auric Goldfinger/Gert Frobe
GOLDFINGER, 1964)

Final words

57

'Do you expect me to talk?'

This movie quote ('Do you expect me to talk?') was voted one of the all-time best in cinema history and number one out of all of the 007 productions. This iconic scene, certainly, in its day, introduced the word 'laser' into most people's vocabulary.

The intrepid secret agent used some good *questioning* techniques and finely targeted '*laser words*' to get out of trouble (and avoid some eye-watering repair bills from his tailor!). We can learn from this type of communication.

I hope that after reading these pages you have become more aware of your own talk. Through habit we've spent a lifetime conducting our talk in what could reasonably be called an imprecise manner. As we've discussed at length, words have power. Words have energy. Words can, and do, change the course of history and therefore the world. In your personal world, change comes from the words you say.

We need to think of developing 'laser' words that hit the target during our interactions – specific, succinct and efficient use of words.

The way we talk to ourselves can be how we talk to others, which might not be as mindful as it can be. It requires awareness not only of how we are communicating with the other person, but how we also communicate with ourselves. As we discussed earlier, consider whether 'screen' based communication would be better served by talk – whether telephone or face-to-face. Get out of the habit of taking the easy option of digital communication when relationships are at stake. I expect you to talk!

Strive to improve your talk with your spouse, partner, family, friends and work colleagues and clients. Once you form your new habits of conversing you can aim for linguistic gold.

Of course, you'll still have disagreements, friction, frustration – and apologies to make. But the point is that you'll have far fewer; and, more importantly, you'll know where you made the poor judgement.

Words can be confusing and can, at times, get in the way of true meaning.

Conversational habits, just like any habit, take a little time to be reprogrammed. Think of those laser-guided words that will help you achieve what you want whenever there's the temptation to talk before *thinking.*

'Watch your **thoughts,** *they become your words*
Watch your **words,** *they become your actions*
Watch your **actions,** *they become your habits*
Watch your **habits,** *they become your character*
Watch your **character,** *it becomes your destiny.'*

So, good luck on your adventure – your adventure with words.

'Do you expect me to talk?' you may ask, to which my response to you is a heartfelt: 'No . . . I expect you to talk – *better.*'

Afterword
by Gillian Tett

We use words without thought, and rarely notice the contradictions they contain or confusions that they can create.

How many of us, for example, have ever thought of the multiple meanings of the short word 'spell' – and the fact that this contains some seemingly unconnected ideas? But Borg's book challenges us to examine the unexamined in a pithy and powerful way.

He dissects the language we use and our style of speech – and then offers a plethora of easy-to-understand pointers for how we can all improve our communication skills.

Fascinating reading for anyone who wants to be more effective in life – in any social group!

Gillian Tett is the US Managing Editor of the Financial Times *for which she also writes weekly columns and her award-winning writing covers a range of economic, financial, political and social issues. She has served in editing and reporting roles in London, New York, Tokyo, Russia and Brussels.*

In 2014, she was named Columnist of the Year in the British Press Awards and was also recognized as Journalist of the Year (2009) and Business Journalist of the Year (2008) by the British Press Awards, and as Senior Financial Journalist of the Year (2007) by the Wincott Awards.

Her book Fool's Gold *won Financial Book of the Year at the inaugural Spear's Book Awards in 2009. With a PhD in social anthropology from Cambridge University, her latest book* The Silo Effect *casts an eye on the global economy and financial system through the lens of cultural anthropology.*

Index

ALSO BY **JAMES BORG**
THE NUMBER ONE BESTSELLER
(*Nielsen Bookscan*: Popular Psychology chart)

PERSUASION

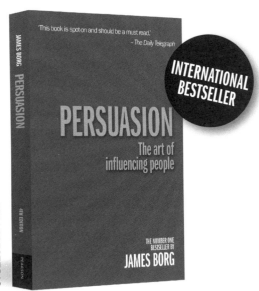

Shortlisted for the:
'800 CEO-READ BUSINESS BOOK OF THE YEAR AWARD' 2009 (USA)
(**Winner** of 'Best of the Rest' award)

Shortlisted for the British Airports Authority:
'BAA BEST NON-FICTION TRAVEL READ AWARD' 2009

Future magazine publication:
'50 BEST BUSINESS BOOKS' of all time (1936–2013)
(one of only three UK authors to make the list)

PRAISE FOR *PERSUASION*

'One of the best selling self-help/popular psychology books of the
21st Century.'
Philip Stone, Charts Editor, *The Bookseller*

'This book is spot-on and should be a must read.'
Dr James Rieley, *Daily Telegraph*

'A rare 'self-help' book – marvellously readable and fun. Hugely to
be recommended.'
Jilly Cooper

'This book should be on every individual's bookshelf.'
Sir John Harvey-Jones

'An indispensable handbook for all of us who need to get other people to
do what we want.'
Sir Anthony Jay, co-creator and writer of BBC's *Yes Minister*

'I'm persuaded that this book is an essential aid to getting people
on your side. Invaluable.'
Sue Lawley, BBC radio and TV presenter

'A witty and fast-paced journey ... There are some real gems in this book.'
***Edge* Magazine**

'Gave me a new-found confidence ... won me £12000 of work ... helped
me gain more friends - all in 3 weeks. Give me more James Borg.
You are a bloody genius!'
Amazon reviewer

'Persuaded? We were. Buy it.'
***Management Today* magazine (Voted 'best of its kind')**

'This is a handy readable guide ... The author persuaded me
to review this book. Damn, he is good.'
Jeremy Vine, *The Times*

ALSO BY **JAMES BORG**

BODY LANGUAGE

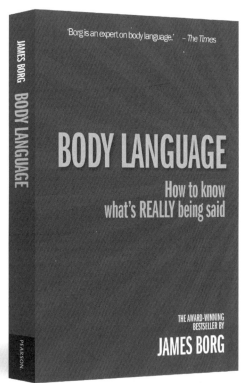

WINNER of BAA (British Airports Authority):
'**BEST NON-FICTION TRAVEL READ AWARD 2009**'
(Voted for by the public)

PRAISE FOR *BODY LANGUAGE*

'Borg is a body language expert.'
The Times

'This book shows you how to use your body language to your advantage.'
ShortList magazine (No 1: 'The Year's Best Business Books 2009')

'Barack Obama was once asked which book he would take to The White House if he became President. His reply was "Abraham Lincoln's"... sadly I couldn't think of any which I held in similar esteem. However, James Borg's book starts to address this situation'.
Supply Management magazine

'I've become an expert in this field since studying Body Language . . . in seven chapters he takes the reader through the shocking ways our bodies reveal boredom, dislike, anxiety, indifference, mendacity – and, in happier moments, liking and even attraction.'
The Independent

'It is definitely a five-star read!'
San Francisco Book Review

ALSO BY **JAMES BORG**

MIND POWER

'*Mind Power* is the best of the current self-help books.'
– *The Guardian*

MIND POWER
Change your thinking, change your life

BY THE NUMBER ONE
BESTSELLING AUTHOR
JAMES BORG

JAMES BORG   MIND POWER

PEARSON

PRAISE FOR *MIND POWER*

'Completes his trilogy with a book packed with power . . . *Mind Power* by James Borg is the best of the current self-help books.'
Guardian

'. . . *Persuasion* and *Body Language* have both been well received and when you read *Mind Power* it's easy to see why . . . intelligent and rational ways in which everyone can get their neurons firing and improve their thinking. Light hearted and enthusiastic style make this one of the better self-help books out there.'
Booksquawk

'I give full credit to James Borg . . . I recommend you read this book in full. It's a potential life changer.'
Life Coach Directory

'An author of inspirational works.'
The Independent

"The world is full of magic
things, patiently waiting for
our senses to grow sharper."

W.B. YEATS